THE PATH OF THE FEATHER

MICHAEL SAMUELS, M.D.,
and
MARY ROCKWOOD LANE,
PH.D.

G. P. PUTNAM'S SONS
New York

THE PATH OF THE FEATHER

A Handbook and Kit for Making Medicine Wheels and Calling in the Spirit Animals

G. P. Putnam's Sons
Publishers Since 1838
a member of
Penguin Putnam Inc.
375 Hudson Street
New York, NY 10014

Published simultaneously in Canada

Library of Congress Cataloging-in-Publication Data

Samuels, Michael.
The path of the feather : a handbook and kit for making
medicine wheels and calling in the spirit animals /
Michael Samuels and Mary Rockwood Lane.
p. cm.
ISBN 0-399-14572-9
1. Shamanism—North America—Handbooks, manuals,
etc. 2. Medicine wheels—Handbooks, manuals, etc.
3. Animals—Religious aspects—Handbooks, manuals, etc.
4. Indians of North America—Religion—Handbooks,
manuals, etc. I. Lane, Mary Rockwood. II. Title.
BF1621.S25 2000 00-036992
299'.7—dc21

Printed in China
10 9 8 7 6 5 4 3 2 1

This book is printed on acid-free paper. ∞

Book design by Amanda Dewey
Map illustration and animal drawings by Jackie Aher

CONTENTS

The Ancient Ones and the Spirit Animals Speak to You 179

The Meaning of the Directions

East is new beginnings and change.

South is the present and manifestation.

West is completion and healing.

North is the unformed and grounding.

Center is power and the essence.

The Meaning of the Animals

Owl is inner vision without fear.

Eagle is illumination, seeing in clarity and light.

Lion is strength, passion, and power.

Bear is healing with responsibility.

Turtle is being grounded in the body
of the living earth.

A very special thank you for your purchase! I am thrilled you wish to own your very own witchy creation from the Studio of Steelgoddess. I have great passion and love for what I do and am over the moon that you find it just as special. Please feel free to contact me if you have any questions.

With Love and Light,
Steelgoddess

Follow me on Facebook!
www.facebook.com/steelgoddess

Serpent is energy rising and rebirth.

Beaver is commitment and building.

Lizard is survival and adaptability.

Coyote is not taking yourself seriously.

Wolf is untamed wildness and beauty.

Dog is loyalty and protection.

Spider is connections, weaving the web of life.

Ant is paying attention and being yourself.

Deer brings spirals of beauty into your life.

Horse is traveling and doing work in both worlds.

Buffalo is abundance and nurturing.

Dolphin is communication and being
yourself without material objects.

Man and **woman** are oneness and the wisdom
of ancient experience. They are female
and male energy, lovers, parents.

The Making of the First Shaman

A hunter named Bo-Khan was married and had a son. He lived in a large, round hut covered with skins. He had everything he wanted, but he was sick. Sad and confused, he had dreams he could not remember, and visions he could not see.

One night a celestial maiden came to him. During the day she lived on earth and was married and had one son, but at night she lived in a dream world in the sky. While he was in his deepest dreams, she flew to Bo-Khan and sang to him. "Bo-Khan, it is time. It is all changed now. I am your fairy spirit woman, your Ayumi. I will make you see and teach you to remember your dreams. I will breathe visions into you each night. I will take you beyond space and time. I am here only to make you a shaman." Each night in his dreams she gave him a vision. She took him on the path of ecstasy, teaching him to celebrate his physical body while flying in visionary space. She taught him to see beyond all obstacles and out of the eyes of the animals.

She seduced him from his body, and taught him to draw out his own soul. She revealed herself to him: a celestial being of a mysterious light. Seeing her gave him an internal light, which enabled him to see in the dark, with closed eyes, things that are hidden from others. Now he could see to the end of the earth.

She flew with him to the seventh heaven, and they had nine spirit daughters. Each one gave birth to a son, and from each son came one religion. From the first son came the race of shamans who could see and hear the spirits, animals, and voices of the living earth.

—adapted from *Shamanism: Archaic Techniques of Ecstasy,*
by Mircea Eliade

Introduction

THE SHAMANIC JOURNEY, the tradition of the medicine wheel, and the voices of the spirit animals all descend from a time when we were more intimately connected with nature. *The Path of the Feather* will provide you with ways to restore that intimacy by offering techniques for drawing taut the sinews that bind us both to the living earth and to our ancestral knowledge.

Using this work, ask for knowledge, for sacred awareness, for guidance. Ask for light and for the results that derive from right action. In response, you will hear wisdom and loving counsel, just as our ancestors did. The benefits of these practices will come to you in ancient ways: through dreams and visions, through trance and Sacred Knowing.

In 1982 *The Book of Runes* midwifed the return of an ancient oracle. It described for travelers the lay of the land and provided a "compass for conduct." While *The Path of the Feather* takes us on a different journey, it leads to the same destination. Use this book as a map, a guide to the sacred space we all inhabit.

The Path of the Feather is a timely and welcome addition to the body of work that carries on the living tradition.

Ralph H. Blum
Maui

WELCOME TO THE PATH OF THE FEATHER

WE THANK YOU for being here. We honor you for who you are and for the work you do. Owl welcomes you, lion welcomes you, bear welcomes you, turtle welcomes you. All the animals of the earth welcome you and invite you to join in this sacred song, this meditation, this prayer.

Along the Path of the Feather we will hear the voices of the living earth; we will make medicine wheels, listen to the spirit animals, and heed the ancient ones. *The Path of the Feather* will teach you to be a contemporary shaman. This book will help you learn to live your daily life as a vision quest, as a shamanic journey. The Path of the Feather makes the empty sacred.

You mark your steps along this path by making medicine wheels. These powerful rituals illuminate and harness the earth's energy. By making medicine wheels, you will know who you are and what you are to do in this life—you will have the power to act and change your world.

In *The Path of the Feather* you will make medicine wheels for three basic purposes: first, to create sacred space and become a shaman; second, to ask questions about your life and solve problems; and third, to manifest what you want. The medicine wheel for each of these purposes is in its own chapter at the end of Section One. Each of these medicine wheels is a type of work, a sacred practice done with intent to accomplish one particular goal. Every time you make a medicine wheel, you actually create sacred space, have questions answered, and manifest your desires, the goals overlap and all are part of the healing of the earth.

This book comes with a kit that will allow you to make your own personal medicine wheel, to create sacred space for honoring your life, your work, and yourself. By doing this ritual you draw your own atlas to sacred space that surrounds you, creating the directions of your life. *The Path of the Feather* kit sets you on your sacred journey to find the path of your own spirit.

This journey is deeply personal, self-generated, and real. At its beginning, you stand, complete with your whole life and history. You come with your visions, the spirit animals you already have, and the ones that exist in your periphery waiting to enter. You may have never seen your visions or met your spirit animals but they are there, deep in the spiritual dimension and in visionary space. Our spirit animals have been with us forever, nurturing us, protecting us, and guiding us.

Along the Path of the Feather, the animals will speak to you; they will call to you—if you listen. By creating your own medicine wheel, you invite them in and ask them to become partners in your vision quest. They will thank you for heeding their voices—voices that have been ignored too long.

This shamanic journey is your personal story of transformation, empowerment, and healing. It need not be a physical journey. It is simply a way of seeing your life—and the earth—as sacred. You will learn to see yourself as a shaman, understand your place on earth, and become aware of your actions. You will tap into the powers of the living earth. By honoring Her sacred space and Her spirit's voices, She will help you to answer the questions in your life and manifest the reality you wish to see. You are ready to embark on your journey now, as you are.

But what else does becoming a shaman mean? How does it pertain to going to work? To marriage? To child rearing? To trauma, pain, and healing? To sickness and health?

The answer will not always be clear. It may come in a moment, or you may find it only much later. But the answer will be the same as it has been for people the world over since time began. The Path of the Feather places you in two spaces at once. Meeting spirit animals through the open door of the medicine wheel gives you a whole new perspective on life. As you walk with us, you'll realize that you are not alone; that the earth Herself is looking out for you; that the animals, spirits, and energies of our world want to help you live your life in harmony. Sometimes you'll have to seek out the answer to your dilemma, and sometimes it will come to you like a bolt out of the blue, in a dream, while staring into your child's eyes, in the midst of watching a friend in pain, in grief.

But you must allow yourself to experience the healing of the living earth—you must invite this beauty in. The ancient shamans teach us how. The medicine wheel is the door you open. In that protected space, you quiet down to hear what the earth is telling you.

This all may seem arcane, even other-worldly, but it was the way of our most ancient ancestors. Maybe it's in our genes, for it's our way, too—most of us just don't know it yet. The Path of the Feather lights the journey we all are on. By its glow, we pick our footing and step with assurance. Without it, we still travel the road, but we stumble and fall.

You already have medicine wheels/sacred spaces/altars—call them what you will—around you. Do you have a flower bed that you labored over? There begins your medicine wheel. How about a stuffed animal that perches on your desk or computer monitor? A power animal just might be staring you in the face. Does your mantelpiece support a cluster of photos? Is there a place you stare off into, or an object you gaze at when you want to quiet the sound in your mind, when you just want to *think*? Yes? Then you already have sacred space in your life. These shrines that you already have make you live in and see the world differently. The Path of the Feather takes you to the places you've been visiting when you've wanted to be "somewhere else" or "thinking" or "meditating" or just "at peace." But now you go there with intent, with wisdom. As you follow this path, notice how many familiar objects in your life are closely linked to the medicine wheel. Notice how many rituals recall the acts you do naturally. Realizing this familiarity will make the exercises seem less foreign, and soon you'll know deep in your cells that you've been on this path forever. With the medicine wheels in this book, you will shift your ability to make sacred space from the unintentional to the intentional.

WHY THIS BOOK IS CALLED *THE PATH OF THE FEATHER*

Out of all the gifts of the animals, feathers are the easiest to find. It takes a special moment, a sacred second, to see the beauty of the feather. If you have paused long enough to notice, and stopped to pick one up, be assured that you are already on the path. If you have never taken the time to pick up a feather, now is the moment for you to begin.

Birds leave their feathers as gifts all around us. You won't find other traces from animals around you as easily, unless you are lucky enough to live in the wild. But right in front of you in the parking lot of the supermarket, right in the street in front of your office, is a feather taking you on this journey. It will fly you to the sacred sites and sing to you of the legends. It will make you come alive and uncover your purpose. Each time you pick up a feather, it is a message that you are on the right path. Each feather is a doorway to sacred space, to the animal who left it, and to the medicine wheel.

How to Make Your Medicine Wheel

This Book Comes from Our Visions

The Animal Spirits Called Us to Write This Book

This book and our understanding of the medicine wheel emerged from the voices of the spirit animals and the ancient ones as we heard them in our visions. Here are the stories of how *The Path of the Feather* was born. As with all things, they are ordinary and mystical at once.

MICHAEL:

"After I left medical research as an immunogeneticist, I was a physician on a Hopi and Navaho reservation. There I met elders who showed me healing rituals. When I returned to California, I set up a wholistic clinic in Bolinas. We had body workers, color healers, imagery therapists, and theater. A powerful healer, Rolling Thunder, came to our clinic and taught me much about healing.

"At that time my spirit animals came to me. In a vision, bear came to me and offered himself as my spirit animal for healing. For me, he was the animal of the west guarding the threshold of my dreams. Although I didn't know it, this bear had traveled with me for many miles. When I took my patients into their healing space, the bear came with us and was my helper. When I healed, he came into me, I became the bear. He was my spirit animal for me when I worked as a physician healer.

"I wrote *Spirit Guides* in 1973 with Hal Bennett, on how to find animal guides for healing. Hal and I taught workshops, and spirit animals became an important part of my work. I taught a workshop with another gifted healer, White Bear Woman, at Hollyhock on Vancouver Island, and we did medicine wheels together and made a sweat lodge. I began to make medicine wheels with the animals to create balance in my healing work. I realized that one animal was not enough and that I needed to have spirit animals around me for more than one purpose. Then I met the bear that would accompany me on my healing journey.

"I had a powerful vision. I was eating salmon while lying on the ground. It was soft and beautiful. The earth was covered with moss and ferns and when I touched it, it echoed like a drum. I looked down, and the earth had become a woman's body. I fed her a salmon. The woman ate the salmon, and then the salmon swam down into the center of her chest. I followed.

"I found myself on a river, became a bear fishing for salmon high in the mountains. With his eyes, I saw. I stood next to a cold, clear river and

looked up at the snow-covered mountains all around me. I pulled salmon out of the river with my claws and ate them. I raised my head, sniffed the air, looked upriver. There was another bear with cubs. She started walking, and I followed her up to the mountaintop. She went up to the highest peak. Here, the light was fractured, refracted as from a crystal. In that fragile light, I could look in all directions and see the whole earth around me. The second bear lent me her eyes and I looked out of them and saw deeply into bright visionary space.

"With this vision, I saw for the first time through the eyes of my spirit animal. Up until then, the bear accompanied me, protected me, but now I merged with him. I was *in* shamanic space, not just looking at it from outside. And as I saw the beam of light through the eyes of the other bear, I realized how powerful this space was for transformation and healing. The bear on the mountaintop showed me that this wisdom is not for me alone but for all who will climb the mountain. From this point, anyone can see the full scope of the world—*if only they care to look.* The bear taught me that I needed to bring the ancient practice of shamanism into a thing of relevance to modern life. The bear gave me the confidence to be a healer, to tackle the toughest cases, to do the unconventional in the drive to make my patients well. But she gave me a responsibility. She demanded in return that I bring shamanism into the modern world so that all who wish to can see with her eyes.

"By 1985, my healing work centered more and more around cancer. As I worked with my patients using guided imagery, they would often ask me to teach them to find their spirit animals to help them heal their cancer. They would ask me for a shamanic initiation so they could heal themselves and heal their lives. For many years, I helped my patients meet spirit animals and taught them to incorporate these animal helpers in the healing process.

"Patients also asked me if they could use the medicine wheels that I had all around my office to help them heal. I began to make medicine wheels with my patients first in my office, and later outdoors. Sometimes we would do large medicine wheels together. I would take a patient with cancer up on Mount Tamilpais; to the springs in the east, the sacred old redwood trees of Muir Woods in the south, the Pacific Ocean in the west, the Miwok village in the north. I would put them in a crater on the mountaintop and cover them with rose petals. We would design our living medicine wheels together and use them as sacred healing rituals.

"My bear vision changed me profoundly; it changed my life and my work. Everything in this book emanates from what I saw as my bear from the mountaintop. *The Path of the Feather* was born from the gift that vision gave to me. Now it is for you. It is your gift. Open your eyes and take it."

MARY:

"I went to Boston College and earned a master's degree as a nurse practitioner in wholistic alternative therapies. In my practice, I used guided imagery. I found when I spiraled down into the imagery with my patients, what emerged was their own inner voice, the voice of their inner healer. Sometimes this was all they needed to heal. I was the witness and facilitator to their own personal healing journey. In my self-exploration, I did moon circles and went into the sacred springs near my home. That is where I was taken by the owl. Then I could see out of the eyes of the owl.

She led me to the sacred sites, the oasis, the ceremonial mounds. Here is my mystical story of being taken.

"One evening I was waiting for the full moon to rise. I was alone in a group of ancient oak trees in the center of the prairie. I stood under a giant ancient oak tree to watch the sun set. The sun filled the entire horizon as it set, leaving streams of gold and orange and purple. Its brilliance was magnificent.

"Now it was dark and difficult to see, but the old grandmother oak was beside me. Suddenly a gigantic owl with a huge wingspan swooped down and hit me on the back of my head. As I fell to the ground, I felt myself taken to the highest tree. I could see over the treetops and down into the sacred grove. In the center were eight oak trees forming a ring. They were a spiral, an ancient vortex of energy, whirling like a spring from the earth. I felt the water, air, earth, and fire all blend in making the world. In each tree was an owl and as they looked down at my body, they took flight and brought me into the sky. I saw that I was the whole sky reaching across the horizon. It felt as though I had become the very heavens. The stars and galaxies now filled my own body. The owl had taken me.

"Suddenly, I was back in my body, my face in the grass, my hair covered with leaves. I was back on the earth clenching the grass, frightened. 'Oh, my, did the owl think I was its prey?' I looked up as a huge harvest moon came over the trees and the whole oak grove became illuminated. I saw the ring of eight trees and from each tree an ancient spirit came out to meet me. I could feel them. They were the ancient ones. They looked like owls and humans at once. After the vision ended, I looked down at my feet and noticed an owl feather. I picked it up and held it in my hand.

"I realized that I could see out of the eyes of the ancient ones and see where they walked. Through them, I rediscovered the ancient mounds and ceremonial sites around my home. I could see them in the landscapes. I could see how the animals had once lived. So I walked in the footsteps of the ancient ones and saw how the world once was. I heard their stories.

"This vision changed my life. Seeing through the eyes of the ancient ones and seeing the ancient spirits changed my way of viewing reality. It allowed me to rediscover places of power and to connect with a spiritual strength and energy that became the backbone of my work in the modern world. All my future work was a shamanic practice that was given to me. With this new vision I could weave the tapestry of my life. The ancient ones work with me to manifest their vision on earth. The spirits of the ancient trees teach me how to make each act I do a right action for healing and saving the earth.

"Then, in the Arts in Medicine program that I set up at Shands Hospital (University of Florida), I met artists who were healers already on their own path. The artists were on shamanic journeys rediscovering ancient healing practices of music and dance. I earned a Ph.D. in nursing at the University of Florida with my thesis on how art heals. I took the artists on retreats to ancient sacred sites to nurture their work. We made medicine wheels together and called in spirit animals to help the artists work with the children and adults in the hospital. I took artists down crystal blue rivers, into the sacred springs and into old trees, and we did ceremonies.

"*The Path of the Feather* was born from the gift the owl feather gave to me in my mystical vision. Now I share it with you. It is your gift. Hold out your hand and take it."

Retelling Your Life as Your Vision Quest

We relate these stories of our ordinary lives and our mystical visions—one no less real than the other for having been imagined—to illustrate how ordinary people looked back on their lives and saw that they had been on a shamanic journey all along. You can retrace your life history to see your own shamanic path. Perhaps you can recognize the mystical visions that made you and reshaped your ordinary story as a time line of your shamanic vision quest.

You will see that everything you do, whether you are a teacher, a doctor, a stockbroker, or a nurse, can be retold to define the sacred path you have already traveled. Retelling your life as your vision quest reconstructs your own reality. Along the Path of the Feather, you will take your own life and reframe it as a vision quest. Looking back on your life as a shamanic vision quest changes who you are now and who you will be in your future.

A woman was confused about who she was and what she wanted to do. She was a successful surgeon, and all who knew her thought she had the perfect life. But to her, life was a jumble. There were many strands of her life that did not connect, and she felt that she was something different to everyone. She was torn apart, as job, children, and self all competed for her time and attention. It seemed to her that she had done many things in her life that were unrelated or wasted. She had gone to medical school and become a surgeon; she had fallen in love and started a family; she had studied meditation, theosophy, prayer. How could she tie these strands together? How could she make them work together?

A shamanic understanding of her path made things clearer. Through dreams and visions, through ritual and listening to the stories all around her, the woman began to see each strand of her life weaving into the other. She was a healer. A healer of her patients. A healer of her family. A healer of herself. All needed her attention, and all needed healing, but seeing her life as a vision quest showed her that by tending to her patients, she healed her family and herself. By loving her family, she mended her patients and her life, and by caring for herself, she healed all whom she touched.

As you re-story your life, look at your years of study, look at the pieces, the strands that make you who you are on your sacred vision quest. Let the medicine wheel be the place where these strands come together. Let it be the point from which they are spun into the web of your life. When you make the medicine wheel, you realize that all paths have led you to this point. They have all led you back to your heart.

Once a person sees himself as on a shamanic path, his future is different. A land developer decides to make a shopping mall, but he is on a shamanic path. Before, he saw land only as a means to making a profit. He saw the mall, the parking lot. Now he sees the sacred living earth and connects to the spirit animals. He will create a different project; create an ecosystem; make places for animals, trees, water. He will honor the flow and energy of the earth as he builds, and he will reap the rewards of it—in his own life, in his family's life, and in his community.

Living your life as though you are on a sacred path will make you shamanic; it will let you walk in the tracks of the ancient ones. The ancient ones knew that becoming a shaman is a lifelong goal, however. At the end of this book, you will find a shamanic initiation—a ritual you can follow to bind your fate with that of the ancient ones. After that, the learning will have just begun. This will make you a shaman.

The Path of the Feather is a true path to becoming a shaman. Each medicine wheel you will make takes you one step further on the path. By making medicine wheels, you embody sacred space in your life. The spirit animals will come to you and help you see who you are and what you are to do. The vision quest oracle will answer questions and guide you in the decisions of your life. You will be connected to your spirit animals and your life will be transformed into a life that is shamanic. By making sacred medicine wheels, you will be able to change your life to manifest what you desire.

About the Path of the Feather Kit

By now you have taken the first steps. You have opened yourself to that which you may have earlier dismissed. But the time has come for you to meet the companions you will have on this journey. Consider these as only introductions; you will come to know these concepts better as we walk together.

Definitions

A *shaman* is a person who has a visionary experience that he or she cultivates and uses as a way of knowing how to do right action in the world. The shaman brings the spirit animals to the world. The shaman then takes the visions from the mystical world and manifests them in the community and into physical space and time for healing.

A *spirit animal* is a synthesis of all the animals of that species that have lived in the present, past, and future. The spirit animal has the wisdom, strength, and energy of the animal and teaches you the essence of what the animal is. A spirit animal is connected to the actual animal while being far greater than any one animal.

A *vision quest* is a pilgrimage—physical or mental—to sacred sites or doing sacred work to find visions to direct your life. Throughout history, people have embarked on vision quests, going out into nature to hear the stories of their lives. On a vision quest, you meet your power animals who tell you your story and give you the strength to be who you are.

A *medicine wheel* is a sacred place that aligns you with earth. It helps you to identify the directions so you can be grounded and oriented in sacred space. It is your gateway into the visionary world. The medicine wheel calls the spirit animals to you. Through its space, they become your guardians and guides and bring you your sacred visions. The medicine wheel is your map for the journey ahead.

Healing is being in balance and harmony. It is being conscious and awake to the beauty of nature. We are healing when we give birth to the spirit animals in the world. As we see out of their eyes and listen to their voices in the medicine wheel, our bodies, minds, and spirits are renewed by the natural healing energy of the living earth.

About the Kit

Your *Path of the Feather* medicine wheel kit gives you all the tools you need to implement the Path of the Feather in your life immediately.

Take out the pieces of the kit. You should have a medicine bag, thirteen shaman wooden stones, a medicine wheel map, and a compass. The shaman stones have small figures of animals drawn on them that represent:

- owl-eagle
- coyote-wolf-dog
- lion-cat
- spider-ant
- bear
- deer-horse
- turtle
- buffalo
- serpent
- dolphin-whale
- beaver
- man-woman-child
- lizard-alligator

The figures carved on the stones are deliberately indefinite. They can stand for one animal or several animals. For example, the owl-eagle stone can be an eagle, an owl, a hawk or whatever bird you wish. The shaman stones are ancient tools for touching and embodying the energies of the spirit animals. Peoples have used carvings, fetishes, or totems to bring the visions of the spirit animal into the physical world and to make them visible to everyone.

The compass allows you to orient to the directions within your medicine wheel. The medicine wheel map is a sacred space on which to build your medicine wheel. The spiral pattern on the map is grounded in the earth with a feather just as the Path of the Feather grounds you in the spiral of your own sacred work.

The medicine bag holds the shaman stones and the compass. You can also use the medicine bag for sacred gifts from the earth such as the first feather you find on your journey. Eventually bones, rocks, crystals, and stone animals you buy or are given go into the medicine bag too. For most people, Zuni fetishes or other more elaborate animals join the original carved stones as they journey along the path.

This kit enables you to build a medicine wheel and embark on the Path of the Feather. It will grow and change with you. Your medicine wheel will be completely original, illuminating your path. You may leave this map behind, add—and lose—stones, and change your medicine wheel a thousand times. You can build a medicine wheel around your work, as a ritual, or when you ask a question in your life—no matter. This medicine wheel remains yours forever. Like the spirit animals, it is all the medicine wheels—all the change and growing—of your past, present, and future all in one spot. It is your prayer. It is the act you do to invite change in your life. When you build your medicine wheel, you create a new sacred life filled with wonder and energy.

With These Three Steps Begins the Journey of a Lifetime

Making the Medicine Wheel

The first step on the Path of the Feather is making a medicine wheel and making your life sacred. The medicine wheel is an atlas for your primary orientation in sacred space and time, just as an atlas orients you to travel in physical space. By creating the medicine wheel purposefully, you will begin to feel sacred energies for change in your life. This step is about grounding.

Hearing the Earth's Voices

The second step involves hearing the ancient spirits sing and seeing out of the eyes of the spirit animals in order to understand the earth's story. Now you begin to find your own spirit animals and ancient spirits. They will tell you a story. They are the voices of the vision quest. Seeing out of the eyes of the spirit animals and the ancient ones gives you their power and knowledge. This step is about embodiment.

Finding a Feather

The third step along the Path of the Feather is actually picking up feathers. In this step you see a feather, pick it up, and put it in a medicine bag or in your hair or in a pocket. The act of stopping and picking up the feather is deeply important. Each time you pause, you stop your habitual way of seeing. You stop the rush and you enter sacred space. This simple action is a continuous reminder of being on the Path of the Feather. Each time you find a new feather, you have a new reminder that you are on the right path. This step is about manifestation.

This whole process transforms you into a shaman, reframing your life as a vision quest. You are already on the Path of the Feather.

How to Use This Book

There are no dogmatic solutions in the Path of the Feather. It is a mystical path spinning spirally, changing. Your path will be yours, not ours. Making a medicine wheel is your process, one you will do your own way. Start by following our instructions, but if another way comes to you, follow your way. This is about the living earth speaking to you.

If you wish, you can begin immediately by making the instant medicine wheel in the next chapter. However, to build the medicine wheels, start with preparing to make your first medicine wheel on page 52. There you will find general information on where to build the medicine wheel, how to go into sacred space, and how to give thanks and call in helpers. Next, read the directions of the compass on page 89, because knowing the character of the directions is essential to the process. The instructions for making the medicine wheels for sacred space, asking questions, and manifesting what you want begin on page 93 with the medicine wheel for sacred space, the vision quest oracle, and the medicine wheel for manifestation.

As you make the medicine wheel, read the stories of the animals at the back of the book, beginning on page 181. These stories give you the information you need to interpret the medicine wheel—to understand what your medicine wheel means. You also can refer to the chart on the meaning of the directions and the animals at the beginning of the book (page viii) to guide you as you build each medicine wheel.

In addition, the Path of the Feather has instructions for meeting your own spirit animals and listening to the ancient ones. Try the exercises to meet your spirit animals and see out of their eyes. You also can do the exercises on the vision quest, the shamanic initiation, and bringing in the light. Finally, there are exercises on making large medicine wheels in nature. Start where you want to, do what interests you most, let your heart tell you how to walk the Path of the Feather in grace.

How to Make an Instant Medicine Wheel and the Teachings of the Feather

As you gather feathers, you will literally create a path of feathers. This path is like the Japanese temple paths made of large stones that stand a foot above the earth, each placed several inches apart. When a monk steps on each stone, he must pause a moment and then lift up his leg and step on the next one. The monks go deeper into sacred space with each footstep, with each pause. Each stone is its own place occupying its own sacred place on the earth.

Each feather you find represents a place to pause. When you pick up the feather, you stop and, for a moment, you are taken out of time. In that moment, a message can come to you if you ask for it, and the message is unique to that particular feather. On the Path of the Feather, one feather leads you to another and each tells you part of your story. Put together, each part makes up the story of your life as a shaman. This is your Path of the Feather.

How to Hear a Feather Speak

The feathers speak to you in vision space. They speak as you pick them up. To hear a feather's message, be quiet, pause, and listen. Each feather has a unique message for you. One feather told us, "A feather is given to you. You cannot look for it and find it. It is given as a gift. It comes in a moment when you don't expect it. You can look for them but soon you forget and think about something else and that is when they appear. Suddenly in front of your feet is the most beautiful feather and it takes you from your ordinary thought to the place of no time, of expanded time, and you are there."

When you stop to pick up a feather there is a pause, a taking out of time, and a choice—a choice to act to pick it up. Had you chosen otherwise, you would have missed the moment. Another feather speaks, and its message says, "Wait for a feather to come and then grab the moment and put it in your medicine bag and value it."

With each feather, you are given a gift, a piece of the living earth. What is the gift you give back? It is the giving of yourself to the earth. To those who inhabit her. We offer ourselves. We offer our lives. With each gift you receive, you gain more to give back, and the cycle of abundance goes on. When you find a feather, you know you are on the right path.

Making the Medicine Wheel

Let us walk along the first steps of this path together. Let us make your first medicine wheel. As you read on, the process will deepen and you will understand it better. Your first medicine wheel will be the beginning of your work, your doorway to a new shamanic life.

This wheel will introduce you to the meaning of the directions, the stories of the animals and the energy of the medicine wheel. In this wheel you will place the animals in the directions on the map and then read their stories. This is your getting-acquainted wheel. Each medicine wheel you build will introduce you to different animals until you will know the animals well. But never well enough. We still read the stories after years of working with animals because, like a photograph, they reveal different things with each viewing.

- Choose a place that is beautiful, convenient, and uncluttered for you to set up your first medicine wheel. Choose a place that is large enough for the map, a place that is protected from pets and young children. It can be a tabletop, a dresser, or even an area on the floor.
- Say your own prayer of thanks or use our prayer on page 54. Lay the map on the site you have chosen, and put the compass in the center. Rotate the map under the compass until the picture of the earth points north. The picture of the wind and the sunrise is now in the east, the picture of the fire and the full sun is in the south, and the picture of the water and crescent moon is in the

west. Take the compass off the map and put it next to the map so you can still see it.

— Take all the figurines, and lay them face up next to the map so you can see the embossed figures. In this first medicine wheel, the animals we have used in our medicine wheels for ten years will guide you. They have come to you for this book and are full of power. However, if another animal attracts you, or you have a spirit animal already, you may use that animal in this first medicine wheel. As time goes on, all the animals in the medicine wheel will be yours.

— Close your eyes and let yourself relax. Feel a comforting blanket of love come down on you, like a mist that falls over you like the morning dew. Let it fall on your animal stones and bring out the sacred nature of each one. Touch each stone and hold it to your body, asking that it will be your connection to the animal spirits. Ask the animals to come to you and to be helpers for you and the earth. Ask that they heal you and inform you of who your are and what you are to do.

— Place the owl in the east, over the picture of the wind. The owl says to you, "This is the beginning, there is change in the wind and the air. The sun rises in the east and it is about inner vision. You now have the ability to look deep inside yourself without fear.

— Place the lion to the south over the picture of fire. The lion says to you, "This is about manifestation, your power and passion, and falling in love. The energy of this direction is fire and the fullness of the sun at midday. As you face south, feel your own inner strength and power, for the lion is within you.

— Place the bear in the west over the picture of water. The bear says to you, "This is about healing and letting go. Deep in the waters of your emotions and the unconscious are your dreams and visions. Here flow your healing energies. The sun sets in the west and gives you faith in the darkness of uncertainty.

Place the turtle in the north over the picture of the earth. The turtle says to you, "You are grounded in the earth, in your family and work. This is where the sun shines in shadow. It is the place of the unknown and mystery, but here the universe spins and spirals around you.

Place the human figure in the center of the circle over the picture of a person. The ancient ones say to you, "Your body is your spiritual home. The center of the medicine wheel holds your essence. We will help you and guide you from the center of the medicine wheel."

Place the remaining animals anywhere you want to around the circle wherever they seem to go (see illustration). These animals guard your wheel, standing as sentinels in this sacred space. The animals say to you, "We surround you with love, we are here to nurture and guide you. Our bodies and our visions are the vision of the living earth."

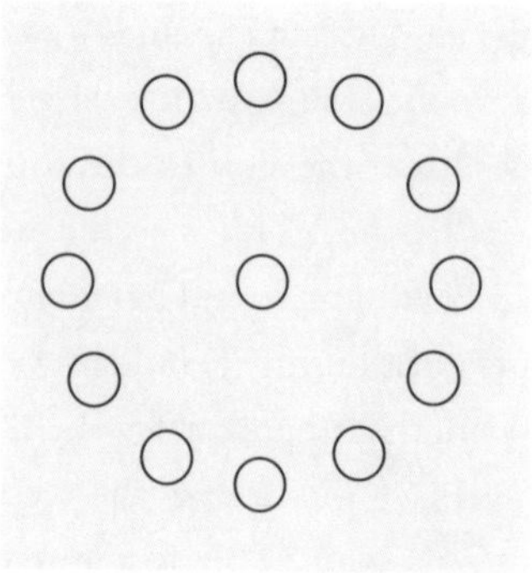

This medicine wheel reading has five components that involve the directions, the animals or ancient ones, the energies, meanings or life patterns, the elements, and the themes. This is our reading of this medicine wheel. It is our invocation—one we recite with you—as we begin this journey. You may have a different reading, but it is no less true, no less honorable.

In the east, which represents change, we placed the owl, eagle, or hawk. The element is air—we go on a spiritual flight. East is the direction of change in our life; in the east we ask, "How can change make us grow?" Imagine the owl in the east flying into the spirit world. She takes you with her. As you enter the visionary space, you will have images of great change in your life.

In the south, which represents love and passion, we placed the lion. The element is fire—the lion urges us to have meaningfulness in all that we manifest. In this reading, the lion in the south provides us the energy to wake up in the morning and begin our work. The lion in the south is about falling in love and about our passion for anything we want to do. In the south, we ask, "How can passion make us grow?" The lion in the south is about love, manifestation, and meaningfulness.

In the west, which represents the unconscious, we placed the bear. The element is water—there is healing from the source. West is the direction of the medicine bear, the traditional animal of healing. It is where our imagery and dreams come from; it is the direction of our unconscious. The west holds the depths of our visionary space and power. In the west, we ask, "How can illness and healing help us grow?" The bear in the west is the watcher, the healer, the controller of this medicine wheel.

In the north, which represents grounding, we placed the turtle. The element is the earth—there is embeddedness in being here. North is the direction of grounding in our work, families, home, and children. At the same time it is about the earth as our Mother. Here we are at once deeply within Her body and our lives. In the north, we ask, "How can grounding make us grow?" The turtle in the north relates to our house and our deep home within the body of the earth. She goes inside the void and brings our prayers out, full of the energy of the living earth.

In the center, which represents spiritual ascendancy into the Goddess realms, we place a woman, the corn maiden. Here there is peace above to rest and be totally loved. Here there is the heart of the universe, feminine power, your essence as Mother, the birth realms, and the essence of who we are when we are perfectly loved. The center is the direction of the deepening process, the creator, the power of the visions, giving birth, and experiencing death. In the center, we ask, "How can She help us grow?" She lives and shows Herself to us from the center.

Every time we make our medicine wheel, our lives change, grow, and become Her gift.

Invite your first medicine wheel to begin to change your life. Invite it to make sacred space and make your life a sacred vision quest.

Great Spirit, make this medicine wheel sacred.
I come with an open heart.
I will accept what comes to me.
I give my life as an offering.
Make my life a sacred vision quest.
May the spirit animals come.
May the powers of the directions come.
May the powers of the elements come.
May my life begin to change
So I bring harmony and balance

To Her, the sacred earth.

Ask a question and let the answer come to you from an animal in the wheel during the course of your day as a thought or idea. You can ask for something to come to you, and let the animals bring instructions on how to find it. They will come throughout your day. You can ask for protection for those you love. Finally, you can ask for guidance in doing right action.

I call forth
To hear the voice of the earth
As Her song.
My I quiet my life
to listen;
May I pause my life
To behold;
May I open my heart
To grace.
May I close my eyes
To see deeper;
May I invite spirit animals into my life.
May I honor the ancient ones so they may be seen;
May I offer my life as a shaman
As I journey on my vision quest.

May I silence the noise so I can hear.
May I close my eyes so I can see deeply.
May I be still so I can behold the spirit animals.
May I open my heart to be in grace.

May I walk on the shamanic path.
As I seek my own visions.

Behold the spirit animal over my heart;
Feel the grace of the earth's spirit.

Go on with your day and watch what gifts come to you. Remember that you are within the sacred space of your medicine wheel, and go where you are guided. Look around you for animals that appear, for a feather under your feet.

Now that you have made your first medicine wheel you are on the Path of the Feather. The animal spirits are your companions and teachers now. They are with you. The animals live within the earth. Their time is your time in the past, present, and future. The animals share the Path of the Feather with you. Owl thanks you, lion thanks you, bear thanks you, and turtle thanks you for inviting them into your medicine wheel and listening to their voices again.

A Prayer of Thanks

In many traditions, shamans pray before they do any sacred healing work. They say it is necessary to call on the powers they believe in and give thanks before starting out.

In the Path of the Feather, we use many terms for spirit: God, Great Spirit, Her. These are all names shamans use for the spiritual force. This way of speaking about the deity simply honors the spirit you believe in. We want to honor all concepts of divinity. The spirituality of the Path of the Feather is inclusive, not exclusive. We believe God has many manifestations of spirit force and speaks to each of us in His or Her own way.

In this book we often call the feminine face of God "Her." She is the blessed mother, the Goddess, the female bear shaman. She is the holder of feminine energy and power. She is also Mother Earth, the spirit of the living earth, who calls to each of us to become a shaman, take responsibility and heal the earth and Her animals.

She is also "She Who Gardens Us from Above." Just as we tend the plants in our gardens and fields, She tends our lives. We are planted in the living earth, awaiting Her ministrations.

We invite you to envision your own deity or spiritual belief when we say "Great Spirit" or "Her." You can invoke Buddha, Great Spirit, God, Jesus, nature, a river, an animal, any force that you believe in. You can say this prayer to yourself or recite it out loud. Say it where you will build your medicine wheel or at any sacred place. Close your eyes, relax, see what it is you pray for.

As we start on the Path of the Feather, let us pray to those who help us on the way. Let us call for them to come to us, and be with us in this sacred work we are about to do. Great Spirit, God, Jesus, Buddha, our Teachers, She who gardens us from above, come to us and help us with this work. We thank you for the earth, for our families, and for us as the shamans that we all are. We thank you for our spirits and our ability to make this prayer. We thank you for our ability to make medicine wheels, to see visions and to speak to spirit animals and ancient ones. We thank you for our eyes, our ears, our hands, our bodies, and our lives.

Great Spirit, help us tell the truth and help us understand these words. Help us make our sacred medicine wheel to know who we are, to receive Her gifts, to act in Her behalf. Give us the power to live with right action. Help us receive the gifts from Her that we wish for, that will balance our lives and the earth. Help us receive the answers to our questions that will inform us on our path and make us true. Help us see, hear, and act with purity of vision and purity of action, to heal ourselves, others, and the earth.

Now pause a moment and be silent. Center yourself. Thank the powers that you believe in. Look at who you are and what you are to do. Pray for what you need. Ask for your questions to be answered. Go in peace. Now we can begin our sacred work together.

The ancient ones say to you, "Do this work with commitment, acceptance, and honor. We bless you in your sacred work."

Shaman, Spirit Animal, and Medicine Wheel

Why Is Shamanism Important Today?

In the modern world, the shaman and her world—vision quests, spirit animals, ancient spirits, and medicine wheels—give us ways of looking at the world to understand it better. The shamanic model has been one of the most powerful ways of looking at creation and how the world is formed anew with each breath. But it is only one model. All religions have their own. Although it is a model, we believe it is very real. The shaman is, and was, the one who took Her visions and voice and made Her reality happen on earth. We use shamanism because this is the oldest recorded way of seeing inward into Her visions and bringing them outward to heal. It is an earth-driven spirituality that honors the animals, the animal spirits, and the living earth.

What Is a Shaman?

One of Michael's teachers, Rolling Thunder, told him this story. Rolling Thunder was up in the mountains, watching a road being built. The road was next to a sacred tree that was the grandfather tree. The plants spoke to him. He knew that the tree was not to be touched. There was a bulldozer there that was about to push down the tree. In his mind, he said a prayer, and the bulldozer stopped. The bulldozer did not work the next day or all the next week. He kept praying. The road was delayed; the ancient tree was saved. Rolling Thunder said, "This work is very powerful. It can change the weather, it can save a forest, it can stop a bulldozer."

That is the power of a shaman.

The shaman is the man or woman who sees into the sacred world. The shaman goes inward and brings his or her visions of the ancient spirits and spirit animals outward to the world as ceremony and ritual. By this process, most similar to prayer, imagery, and art, the shaman heals himself, others, and the earth. By having visions of healing, and by doing sacred rituals, the shaman makes the visions come true. The shaman goes into the world of the spirits and can act there. The shaman can affect the spirits, talk to them, and have them as helpers, or if they are a cause of illness, retrieve the soul. That is how the shaman heals.

In the shamanistic model, the shaman manifests reality in the outer world from the visions in the spirit world. The shaman acts as Great Spirit did when the world was created from Her vision. We are all Her vision on earth. When we become contemporary shamans, we make the world anew. We become who we are deeply, and like the shamans of old, our actions become healing to ourselves, others, and the earth.

The shamanic tradition is believed to have started in Siberia four thousand years ago and then spread all over the earth. There have been shamans on every continent and in almost every culture. No one people owns the term *shaman,* for it is the term for the spiritual healer of any people. As Mircea Eliade, a history of religion scholar, said, "The shaman is the specialist in the soul."

For us, shamans are people who see the beauty in Her light, instead of seeing the darkness in their own fear. Then they help other people see this light and share it to heal.

What Is a Vision Quest?

A vision quest is a search for the images in anyone's life that will heal them and make them whole. In traditional cultures, young people were sent into nature to listen to the voices of the living earth. The elders taught them to go on vision quests to find their path in life and to find their spirit-animal helpers. The person on the vision quest spent days in caves, on mountaintops, on rivers, in the desert. They waited and invited the voices of the spirit animals to come to them. When they heard the voices and saw their vision, they would return to their people and know who they were and what they were to do. Many cultures believed that without the visions seen on such a quest, a person could not function in the world and was not an adult and was not complete. We hope traveling along the Path of the Feather will evoke a similar initiatory experience for you in our contemporary culture. When you know who you are and understand your purpose, you are healed and at peace. You are effective in making the life you want and healing the earth.

A man in deep crisis with his direction in life was traveling with his family in England. They went to see the ancient sites. At the stone circle in Avebury, the man found himself strangely introspective. He went deep into himself and walked around the huge circle of stones, unconsciously making a medicine wheel. As he walked, he touched each stone and wondered about his life. The stones spoke to him. For the first time in years, he knew which direction to follow. *I am doing the right thing,* he thought. *I will take a year off from work and travel all over the earth. This is my time to find myself.* The message from the stones gave him trust in who he was and what he was about to do.

WHAT IS HEALING?

Healing returns us to a balance of harmony, grace, and beauty. Healing promotes creation, rebirth, death, and life, and the manifestation of the spirit animals in the natural and spirit worlds. When there is healing, power is renewed within you and outside of you. Healing is the antithesis of blind destruction. Healing happens when you walk upon the earth, seeing out of the eyes of the animals. If you can see the world through the eyes of the animals, you will understand the harmony and balance of nature and not be blind to the destruction of the earth's body.

She was a physician who worked with cancer patients. She was a skilled professional, but still she felt something was missing in her life. So she made a medicine wheel to ask how to improve her way of caring for people. In the medicine wheel, the bear came to her. The bear derived her healing power from the unconscious, from dreams and visions. The physician realized that when she was one with the bear, she could take on the bear's power to heal. She learned about the bear's having responsibility and holding sacred space and power. The next day, she went on her rounds. Before she entered a patient's room, she closed her eyes and said a prayer for the bear to come with her and help her be a powerful healer. She let the bear drift into her body, and when she saw her first patient, she was surprised at the difference. She felt strong, confident, and powerful. She was able to give her total attention, and her presence amazed her. She could feel and sense things about her patient that she never had known before. She felt a powerful sense of healing energy in her hands, and saw her mission as sacred.

Healing also is about the resonance of body, mind, and spirit, and about your connection with the earth. When the spirit awakens and is seen by the mind, when the visions of the spirit animals are seen and their voices heard, we are healed deeply. We find out who we are and what we are to do on earth in harmony with the earth's body.

What Is a Spirit Animal?

A spirit animal or power animal is the manifestation of the spiritual energy of that animal on earth. The spirit animal is greater than any one actual animal. It embodies the essence of all those animals, all who have come before and all who are yet to be. It is not an anthropomorphized form of the animal, or a human dressed as an animal, it is the animal spirit itself. For example, a spirit bear is the voice of all the bears that have ever lived. It is the bear that can see itself and speak to you. A spirit animal appears to the shaman as a vision. It is the voice of the wild, the voice of nature, the voice of the earth. This animal informs the shaman of the earth energy it tends, and lends the shaman its power and protection. It is a helper that assists the shaman on the journey inward. No shaman would attempt an inner journey without the help of a spirit animal because without one the shaman would be lost. The spirit animal guides the shaman and conveys the energy needed to heal. The spirit animal gives the shaman gifts of sight and teachings of knowledge. The spirit animal gives the shaman protection and wisdom.

Who Are the Ancient Ones?

The ancient ones or ancient spirits are the embodiment of the ancient peoples of the earth. Ancient spirits speak in the collective voices of the ancestors, of the ancient peoples. They are the spirit guides, the inner voices of people on the earth. Ancient spirits are archetypal visions given form. They appear to the shaman in visions to give them messages from the earth. Initially you may see them from afar but eventually they show themselves, speak and make themselves known to you. As they feel more welcome, their voices become clearer. Withdraw from them, and they will grow silent. Cultivate them and the spirits will bring you back into forest, deeper into nature as they take you on their ancient paths.

What Is a Medicine Wheel?

A medicine wheel is a way of creating a sacred space. Throughout history, medicine wheels have been built to hold ceremony, mark sacred space and time, and consecrate a place for ritual. A medicine wheel makes sacred space more real and more visible. Ancient peoples believed that the medicine wheel itself held great power and helped create change and healing. Medicine wheels were circles that were made all over the world. They come from the most ancient cultures and remain alive today.

In many medicine wheels, each direction is associated with a particular animal and/or one type of energy. For example, in our medicine wheel, we place the owl in the east for change and the beginning; we place the lion in the south for passion and manifestation; we place the bear in the west, representing healing power and letting go; we place the turtle in the north, for grounding and the unknown; and we place a woman in the center, representing the Goddess and essence. Each person calls in his or her own animals that represent a particular energy and direction. The medicine wheel can be populated by any of the animals that live or have lived around you on the earth.

The medicine wheel is the place where ritual lives; the place where the spirit world intersects with the material one; the place where we step outside of daily stresses, imperfect jobs, troubled teenagers, money worries, and illnesses. The circle of guardian animals walls off this area for us, allowing us to be vulnerable and to drop our guards. Medicine wheels sanctify our space and our lives, and bring us the protection of our guardian animals wherever we go. Shamans are privileged to carry their temples with them. You can call on the spirit guides anywhere and anytime—but they likewise can call on you.

The wheel is a place where two things can exist at once—the material world and the spiritual world—and neither is more real than the other. The shaman can observe and live in each without penalty. That is the power of the shaman. The shaman—by observing, looking, seeing, listening, hearing, and being—sees life and the earth not as they are but *as they want to be.*

Our medicine wheel is built by placing a small object that stands for the animal or its energy in each of the four directions in a circle. The circle can be as small as a hand or as large as the earth. The object can be an animal fetish, a feather, a seashell, or a special stone. It should be something deeply meaningful to you, something you have found or been given as a gift. In the process, a center is also created and another special object can be put there. You are in the center of your medicine wheel too.

By creating the medicine wheel, you make a physical manifestation of the earth's energies. It is a sacred altar that evokes the powers of the earth, creating an atlas of sacred space, a sacred landscape in which we live. The medicine wheel is spinning, like the earth.

Most of the rituals performed by ancient peoples with the medicine wheel are hidden or long forgotten. Most likely, they involved the hunt, rites of passage, the stars, planting, migrations, or the spirits. They were done at a community level and involved huge amounts of energy. Often the making of a medicine wheel involved moving huge stones hundreds of miles, like the making of the pyramids in Egypt. Medicine wheels or stone circles exist from Europe to North America, from Avebury, England, to Chaco Canyon, New Mexico. They were certainly places of great ceremony, places for the gathering of peoples, and were often set apart from village sites. Sometimes they were burial sites and temples, sometimes they were astronomical devices, but always they were sacred.

The sacred sites were often at the intersection of rivers, on mountaintops, in the center of plains between mountains and rivers. Following the rivers, even today, will lead you to ancient medicine wheels on sacred sites. They were often on the high places, a point where the worshiper could see the distant landscape. Sacred sites were often found at intersections of ley lines, energy lines, places where churches, and other later sacred sites were built.

Small medicine wheels were built for healing, fertility, prayer, and to create sacred space. They were made of small animal carvings placed on stones or pieces of wood. They represented the animals sacred to the particular culture, and were believed to be the embodiment of the sacred energy of the directions. In the Path of the Feather we make our small personal medicine wheel in the tradition of peoples throughout history. We follow an ancient path when we build our own medicine wheel.

The Tradition of the Medicine Wheel

For the ancient ones, the whole world was the Path of the Feather. They were born with the animals and had the experience of living with them every day. They lived on the land and loved it and knew its animals. They dressed as bear, as eagle. They used feathers as offerings to speak to their spirits or gods. On our Path of the Feather, we are reconnecting to these ancient traditions.

Many Shamanic Traditions Exist

The spirit animals were different among almost every culture. One group had a bear, another an eagle, another an owl. Each group oriented the animals in different directions, associated them with different colors, and empowered them with different meanings and stories. For one group of people, the owl was the most shamanic animal, for another it was avoided as a symbol of death. For one people, the water was in the west, for another it was in the east. For others, the wind came from the north, for another it blew from the south. Each people in each place in each time had its own shamanic tradition. Our path adheres to no dogma but rather honors all traditions.

Now as people living all over the earth, we need to hear a new shamanic voice from the earth Herself, a voice more applicable to us today. A voice speaking to all people yet tailored to each of us alone. A voice that illuminates our own spiritual path.

Long ago, when the world was one, the medicine wheel had less specific cultural context than it does now. There was a time when we were all one, when we were all one race. In the evolution of our culture we became many peoples with many stories. But before the stories were culturally embedded, there were no stories of separateness. First we were all one, not separate, simply human. The medicine wheel brings us back to the time when we all were connected, standing as one with the air, the animals, with the land.

The History of Shamanism

Shamanism is the oldest tradition of making change in the world for healing from a spiritual space. Mircea Eliade, the renowned history of religions scholar from University of Chicago, defined shamanism as the technique of ecstasy, a concept defined below. In his book, *Shamanism: Archaic Techniques of Ecstasy,* he describes shamanism as a magico-religious phenomenon that originated in Siberia and Central Asia thousands of years ago. The word comes to us, through the Russian, from the Tungusic, "saman." Throughout Central and North Asia, the magico-religious life of society centered on the shaman and even now, the shaman remains the dominating figure, for the shaman is the great master of ecstasy. The shaman is magical in his ability to make change, and religious in that the change comes from spirit.

Ecstasy is the altered state of consciousness most similar to a trance or the imagery state. Eliade said that the shaman commands the techniques of ecstasy because his soul—his essence—can safely leave his body and travel at vast distances. It can penetrate the underworld and rise to the sky. Through his own ecstatic experience he knows the paths to the extraterrestrial regions. The danger of losing his way in these difficult regions is still great, but sanctified by his initiation and furnished with his guardian spirits, a shaman is the only human being able to challenge the danger and venture into a mystical geography.

Shamanism has been around for thousands of years and it has been changing, developing, and adapting to new circumstances and new ideological backgrounds the whole time. There is nothing pure or primordial about any of these beliefs as they exist today. When you become a contemporary shaman you join the ancient tradition and become one in a line of shamans going back before recorded history.

The History of the Medicine Wheel

The term "medicine wheel" was first applied to the Big Horn Medicine Wheel in Wyoming, the southernmost one that still exists. In the classic definition, a medicine wheel is a circle of stones arranged in a particular manner. By that strict definition, there are about one hundred medicine wheels that have been discovered. Virtually each medicine wheel has a unique form; the Big Horn Medicine Wheel consists of a central cairn, or rock pile, surrounded by a circle of stone. The whole structure looks like a wagon wheel laid out on the ground with the central cairn forming the hub, the radiating cobble lines the spokes, and the surrounding circle the rim. The "medicine" part of the name was given by anthropologists to designate their belief that the stone circles were of religious significance to indigenous peoples. Today, the term is used in popular culture in a broader way that includes small circles of animal carvings and large circles different from the classically defined variety.

Some medicine wheels have been found to have been initially constructed some 4,500 years ago as confirmed by radiocarbon dating of bone. It is theorized that successive groups of people added new layers of rock, and some of their arrowheads, from that time until the coming of Europeans. The long period of use and construction of the medicine wheels suggests that they may have served different functions over the years. Anthropologists speculate that the rituals and ceremonies conducted at medicine wheels may have changed over time. It is not unusual for people to regard particular places as sacred, even when religions change. For example, many modern Catholic churches occupy locales that formerly contained ancient sites. Medicine wheels served as ceremonial sites for several thousand years but details of the ceremonies or the religious philosophy that motivated their construction remain obscure. Anthropologists suspect that hunting magic or buffalo fertility might have played a part in the rituals, but the deeper meaning of the medicine wheels has been lost in time. Today indigenous peoples use the medicine wheel in their own traditional ways.

Indigenous peoples all over the world have built stone circles for thousands of years. The larger wheels have survived; the smaller ones have disappeared without archeological trace. The stone circles in Europe are not popularly referred to as medicine wheels, but in *The Path of the Feather* we use the term *medicine wheel* in a much broader way to define a sacred circle. Here we use *medicine wheel* to refer to a sacred circle where ritual, prayer, and ceremony are conducted for change and healing. By making medicine wheels, you join the ancient tradition of healing and become one in the long line of peoples who have performed sacred ritual in this ancient way.

Preparing to Make Your First Medicine Wheel

Choosing a Place

Use the information in this chapter to make all the medicine wheels in this book. We will tell you about finding the place for the medicine wheel, getting into a sacred altered state of consciousness, blessing the stones, praying, and picking your animals. The instructions for making the actual medicine wheels are in the chapters on medicine wheels for sacred space, the vision quest oracle, and medicine wheels for manifestation.

First you must choose the place to build your medicine wheel. Walk around your house and see which places call to you. It is the starting point of your sacred journey. Don't get too caught up in the selection. Thinking too much about this decision will only take the mystery out of it. Let the mystery take you.

Build your medicine wheel in an important spot, where you can honor your sacred work and where it is protected from pets and young children. Build it either where it is seen by other people or, perhaps, where it is hidden. A medicine wheel is like an altar; it is sacred space, and it needs to be a place that centers your spiritual energy. As you move along the path, every place will become sacred, but take care to place your first wheel somewhere evocative of your own sacred energy.

As you move around your house, you may look at it differently than you ever have before. Look for places that have high spiritual energy. If you wish, you can close your eyes and look for places that light up in your mind's eye. They can appear illuminated or come to you as warm or red areas or spirals of light. Finding your first place is spiritual work. It acknowledges that your home is sacred and that you understand its energies.

Alternately, think about those places that are special to you in what seems to be a mundane way. The place where you set up family photos might be the perfect spiritual spot. Likewise, the spot you always seem to stare off into when you're "spaced out" could be sanctified for you already. Any part of your house that's special is a sacred space.

Preparing Your Sacred Place

When you settle on a location, it is time to prepare it for the medicine wheel. To begin, we often burn aromatic sage bundles to cleanse the site and remove impurities. Sage has traditionally been used by first-nations peoples for centuries. You can sage the entire house, if you wish. Light the sage and push its rising smoke to the edges of the room with a feather. Wave the sage in a clockwise spiral and the house will be in a new light afterward.

As we sage the place where the medicine wheel will go, we say a prayer thanking Great Spirit for the day.

> *Great Spirit, I thank you for the day. I ask you to bless my work as I give you this medicine wheel in peace and beauty. I offer my work to you and to the earth. I thank you for letting me make this wheel. I thank you for the bounty of my life. I pray for what I want to happen in my life to take place in beauty and harmony.*

During the ceremony, feel yourself going deeper and deeper into your inner world. Feel yourself concentrating and, in a sense, going into a trancelike state of mind where you are focused and clear.

An Exercise for Going into an Altered State

Relax; take several slow, deep breaths. Now, in your mind's eye, see yourself walking through a tunnel of space and time. Imagine your consciousness originating from the back of your head, behind your eyes. Separate this awareness from your body, which you see moving forward. Feel yourself in an altered visionary state. Feel your body as relaxed and heavy. Your body feels dense. In your mind's eye, see with clarity and perspective. Feel yourself going into a trance; see your vision narrow. Feel time and space expand and fill with energy. Now, open your eyes and make your medicine wheel.

Orienting Your Map to the Directions

Once you pick your place, lay down the medicine wheel map from your kit. Put your compass in the center of the map. Turn the map under the compass until the N on the compass points to the drawing of the earth. The drawing of wind and rising sun should be in the east; the drawing of fire and full sun should be in the south; and the drawing of water and the crescent moon should be in the west.

This is a beautiful thing to do. Spin the map under the compass as the earth spins around the sun. By doing this, the medicine wheel map links to the sacred earth where the medicine wheel is placed. Think of the map as a prayer rug, a meditation pillow, a prayer shawl. Later you can use any cloth or rug you wish, or even the earth itself, depending on where you make your medicine wheel.

By using the map you begin to look at the world differently. With the directions defined, your body is now oriented in sacred space. You can look to the east, to the south, to the west, to the north and know what lies there awaiting you in your visions to come. Open your medicine bag and lay all the animals and figures in front of you face up. Now find a personal object that you value. It can be a piece of jewelry, a feather, stone, bone, anything that has meaning for you. Place this object in the center of the circle as an offering. Give it to the spirits who will guide you in this work as a gift. Tell them, "I give you this offering in thanks. I give you this offering to ask for your guidance in my journey."

Finding Your Dream

The purpose of the medicine wheel is to manifest your intentions on earth. When you make your medicine wheel, think about your deepest interests. Think about your life, your relationships, your work, your hopes, your dreams. Search for one theme to emerge and become dominant. Center and focus on that one thought, holding it in place in your mind. The medicine wheel is your living prayer for the earth to manifest your dream.

A woman had been thinking of moving. After several years in one spot, she had grown to believe that she belonged somewhere else. Every weekend, the woman fled her life in the city and went paddling on the rivers in the countryside. A few weeks earlier, those excursions began to change. Starting then, she spent the time on the river thinking about how she felt "misplaced" in her life. One afternoon, she saw a beaver on the river swimming downstream toward his dam. Over the next few days, she saw beavers everywhere she looked—on the river, on the banks, on the road leading to her house. Then the weekend came again, and off she went to the river. As she drove up the dirt road to the landing, she found a dead beaver next to the little bridge spanning the river. Not knowing what else to do, she picked up the beaver, put it in her kayak, and paddled downriver. Suddenly a white oak caught her attention. It was an endangered tree, old and rare, and she had never seen it before. She landed on the bank and put the beaver in an indentation between the oak and another ancient tree next to it—a natural medicine wheel, she thought later. Having laid the beaver to rest, she closed her eyes and had a vision. It was a vision of home, of happiness, of peace. She thought, *I belong here.* She became the shaman of the river, the beaver shaman, whose job it is to take care of the river. She thought, *I must move here.*

In the days that followed, she drove all over the area looking for a place to live. Nothing was for sale. The land had been owned for generations. Discouraged, she went back to the river—only this time she drove down a small dirt path that she must have overlooked before. At the end of the path, right before it was lost in the woods, a for-sale sign was nailed to a tree. She walked a few paces past the path, into the trees, and found herself standing on a rise overlooking the river. Just below her was the white oak, and in its shadow lay the beaver. She had found her home.

Your life will begin to change as soon as you make your first medicine wheel. As we create the medicine wheels, we become shamans, changing our lives and our consciousnesses, whether we are aware of it or not. In making a medicine wheel, you don't have to do anything but follow the process. The medicine wheel does the rest for you. This process is ancient, the path well worn. The medicine wheel calls the spirits to you and they come as helpers. As this gift enters your life, things will shift, you will see beauty, and the world will speak to you with clarity. The ancient ones speak to those who listen, and you will hear them. It is a direct communication. The voices come from within you, from the animals, from the trees, from the ancient ones, from Mother Earth. They can be heard as literal voices or you might hear the silence inside the silence. They speak to anyone who will pause to listen.

Each time you make a medicine wheel you will go deeper and deeper into a spiritual, embodied consciousness until you eventually discover a quiet space in the center of your heart. It is a space where mankind's consciousness has been before. You will recognize it and know how to get there easily.

Choosing Your Ambiguous Animal

When you choose a stone representing more than one animal, you must decide which animal it stands for. For example if you choose the bird, it could be an owl, eagle, hawk, or any other bird. To determine which animal your stone stands for, look around you. Which animal has come to you in the last weeks? Which animal do you think it is? If you close your eyes, which animal appears, which one speaks to you? Which animal calls to you? Your intuition will provide the answer.

A patient with cancer who had never made medicine wheels or met a spirit animal came to one of our workshops to learn what she could do to heal herself. As she thought about which animal would speak to her, which animal would help her heal, a small mouse came unbidden to her mind. *I am just imagining this,* she thought, but she let her mind roam unhindered. Opening herself up, she watched as the mouse approached her, hesitant and shy. It said, "I am the beginning, the first animal to come to you. I come to you to bring you your new life. I am the one who comes to you to tell you about the larger animals that will come. I come to prepare you for them so you won't be frightened. I am humble and small, and I bring you your new life. I will lead you into your inner world, your new world of healing to find yourself."

The Language of the Medicine Wheel Pattern

In your medicine wheel kit, there are thirteen shaman stones, which coincide with the thirteen lunar cycles. The four directions on your map are tied to the seasons and the time sequence of the rotation of the earth and moon around the sun. In honoring those two celestial systems, you are stepping into the life pattern of the ancient ones. It is your choice now how you live within this circle. You can express yourself in any of the patterns that follow. For now, learn about the patterns. Experiment with them. Learn their language. Later, as we make medicine wheels for sacred space, for manifestation, and for oracular vision, these structures will become more rigid.

You have already made a medicine wheel using the stones in one circle with a center stone. They can also be arranged in a beautiful pattern of two circles, one inside the other. This pattern is very old and is found in cave paintings of many ancient cultures. Eight stones form the outer circle with one at each compass point and one in between the four directions. Four stones form the inner circle with one stone in each direction. Finally we place one stone in the center. When you use all thirteen stones, you create a full medicine wheel, the richest and most complex, but it is also possible to use fewer stones to create simpler wheels. For example, we frequently use only five stones, placing one in each direction and one in the center of the wheel. The stones can be moved and the pattern changed. You can move stones from the outer circle to the inner one. You can lean the outer stones on the inner ones, you can make the circles larger or smaller, even or uneven.

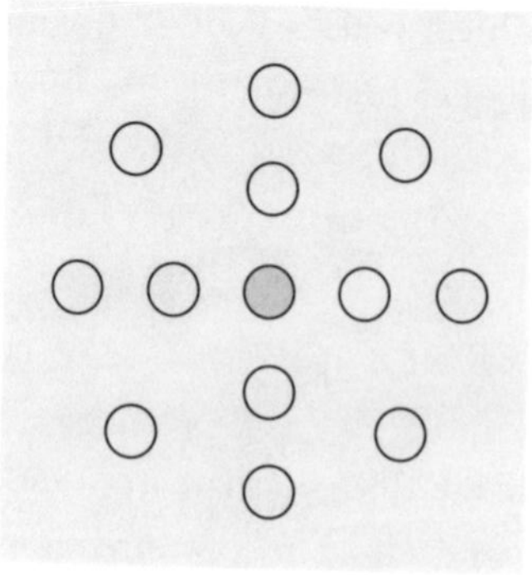

You can experiment with arranging the stones in different patterns. Try arranging the two circles so the four stones make up the outer ring and the eight the inner one. This arrangement emphasizes the four directions as the main focus of the medicine wheel. In this arrangement, the four stones remain fixed even if they are put outside. Or put all thirteen stones in one ring, or twelve in one ring and one in the center. All these patterns and many more were used by people throughout time. None is essential for the medicine wheel to work.

In the medicine wheel, the center stone is you; it is the stone for your life. The center stone also represents the Creator, who is within us and within all things. When we choose the stone for the center of the circle, we become the Creator and we become ourselves. The central stone represents your shamanic life. It is the symbol of what you are manifesting or the focus of the question you are asking.

The inner circle of stones expresses the essence of your sacred journey and represents the immediate voices from Her heart. In the inner ring, you will put four animals, one in each direction. Many people keep the same animals in the inner ring of their basic medicine wheel for years. The animals that people choose come from their experiences in making medicine wheels and from their own lives. People choose animals that come to them, that live around them, whose meanings are important to their life goals. We have instructions for choosing the animals to make your medicine wheel in the chapters on making medicine wheels for sacred space, the oracle, and making medicine wheels for manifestation. We tell you how to meet your own spirit animal in the chapter on meeting your spirit animals. Our animals came to us as we made medicine wheels. They came to us in our outer lives—owl showed herself to Mary, lion appeared in visions, turtle came to us on a road and told us her story, bear came to Michael in visions. When you make the medicine wheel with the same animals they become your friends and allies. They can move within the directions, but they just as often stay in the same place. The animals in the inner ring produce the power of your vision. They make the forms that inform your life. They are the energies that speak to you and that you become.

When the purpose of a medicine wheel is to answer questions, the animals in the inner ring are the ones who bring you your visions. The four core animals will answer depending on where they are living. They will tell a story that will bring out your deepest inner feelings. They will come into your heart and find your wishes and tell them to you in fables. They will take the characteristics of the four directions, their energies and meanings, and bring their stories to you. In a medicine wheel for manifestation, your four inner animals will power your vision with energy to make it happen.

The outer circle of stones is the ring of the guardians. It encompasses the other helpers, including the rest of your friends in your world. These animals can change as your story changes. You might add animals or take some away. You can move them all over the ring, depending on where they fit on a given day. The outer ring animals make your story richer, telling the details of what happens to you each day.

Meeting Your Spirit Animals

There are animals all around us, but the challenge in our world is seeing them through the clutter we have created. Essential to your journey along the Path of the Feather is a quest for the animal. They are the voices of the living earth, and they are calling. Listen, create sacred space for them to feel safe in, and they will guide you.

The Spirit Animals Return

In traditional cultures, the shaman was usually accompanied by spirit animal helpers. They protected him or her and gave the shaman power. They haven't gone away since then, but we've stopped caring for them. They need to be rediscovered.

Finding your spirit animals comes naturally. Perhaps you are wearing an animal T-shirt or have stuffed animals or toy animals around you; maybe you collect animal fetishes or carvings, or have a favorite animal in nature or at the zoo. Perhaps you work to protect an animal or have a pet you love. You may be entranced by an animal in a movie, on TV, or in a book. Any of these animals might be your spirit guides. The animal has been around, waiting for you to call them.

For many, the exercise to meet their spirit animals is pivotal to their lives. The exercise reconnects them with animals they have always had but not recognized. For example, a woman journeyed to meet her spirit animal, and she found an owl. "It did not surprise me," she said, "because I have a picture of an owl hanging up on my wall. It is the only picture in my whole house. My roommate gave it to me. Now I listen for the owls at night. I watch them when I go to the zoo. When I try to talk to my spirit animal, the owl looks directly into my eyes. The first time I met her, she said to me, 'I have been with you. Now you can speak to me. I watch over you. Now you can call me, see me, and know I am there.'"

Like that woman, it is time for you to welcome the spirit animals that have always been with you.

Each spirit animal is a combination of its real animal and its collective spiritual essence. It carries themes and messages that combine with your unique personality. For example, the owl in our medicine wheel has keen sight. It signifies waking up and being seen, emerging from the night, from dreams and visions, and being taken deeper. The owl for us is the combination of the real owl who sees in the dark and hunts, and our vision of the owl as one who helps us see.

The lion for us is about passion, about manifestation, about power and energy. The lion is strong, self-contained, and yet lives in a collective. Brave and fearless, it nonetheless would perish without vast wilderness. The bear for us is about the shamanic journey. The bear is solitary, especially the male. They travel deep into nature and embody intensity. The turtle is about grounding, conservative habits, protection, about lying in the sun, basking in the warmth of life, being an ancient part of the living earth. The snake involves worship, goddesses, the power and energy within you. The rhythm of nature is in each animal. Feel it when the animal comes to you in physical space or visionary space.

Each culture has a different belief about the number of spirit animals and how long they stay with us. In our experience, some people get an animal for life, but for others the animals change. The animals only stay and talk to you if you listen to them. While some people have one animal that is primary, others have many. These choices are up to you and to them.

Meeting Your Spirit Animals and the Ancient Ones

This guided imagery will help you meet your spirit or power animal. Like the ancient ones, the spirit animals come from deep within Her consciousness, and are our deepest memories. We all share DNA with all the animals alive on earth. In our memories, in the memory of our very cells, we can see out the lion's eyes. We are the animals. The spirit animals may be easier to contact than ancient ones, depending on your practice, especially if you have been sensitive to the animal world and its nature. Their voices are louder and they are easier to see. They will come and speak to you when you need them. The animals are helpers and, like the ancient ones, they are guides. They tell you what you need to know. They give you their immense energy. No shaman would ever go into sacred space without his or her animal helpers. This guided imagery exercise can be done to find your spirit animals and to contact ancient ones. Blessings to you in this sacred work.

Close your eyes. Take a couple of deep breaths, letting your abdomen rise and fall. Go into your imagery space as you have many times before. Now put yourself on a path. Feel your feet touch the earth, smell the fresh air, feel the warm breeze on your face. Walk down the path. It goes downhill slightly. The ground is hard and has small stones in the soil. It is solid and secure. Feel the ground and the grass that is on each side of the path. Now the path crosses a wooden bridge across a rushing stream. The bridge has stout railings. You can hear your feet echo on the bridge like a drumbeat as you walk across. Perhaps you need to drop something in the water that you want to get rid of. Do that now.

After the stream, the path now goes upward slightly and comes over a rise. Below you is a large meadow. In the center of the meadow is a grassy circle. Sit in the circle and wait. With you in the circle are your friends and teachers, people who support you in this work. Drift and dream. See the circle become magical, and feel yourself awakening to magic.

Now ask for your spirit animal to come to you. Or ask for an ancient one to appear. You can see behind you, all around you in magic space. Let the animal appear and come up to you. It can come from a distance or appear right next to you. The animal looks like an ordinary animal coming out of the mist. It may appear suddenly or slowly. The animal that appears to you is your spirit animal helper. Let the animal come toward you. It may even begin to speak to you. It will speak in an inner voice that sounds to you like a thought but feels as though it is not yours alone.

You can stay in the meadow as long as you wish. Your spirit animal is part of the earth. It has tendrils that reach deep into the earth, the sky, and you, connecting them all together. If you feel comfortable, let the animal touch you, even come into your body. You can merge with your animal and see out of his or her eyes.

When you are ready, stand up and leave the meadow. The path goes out of the far side of the circle and you can walk down the path farther. It leads to the edge of a forest of old-growth trees. Stand at the edge of the forest by a great ancient tree. Find a tree that beckons to you. Now put your hand on the tree, touch its rough bark. Feel its warmth, its life. Now imagine that when you put your hand on the tree, you move deep into the spiral of your own being. You spiral deep inside yourself, into your heart, and inside your body. Your heart opens with wings. A spirit eye opens within you and sees this experience. It witnesses you becoming the shaman.

Walk back to the meadow, then to the bridge, then to where you are now. Bring your spirit animal. Bring the connectedness with you. Now move your feet. Look around you. You are now on the Path of the Feather. You can see and hear spirit animals. You can hear Her voice telling you how to heal the earth.

A man told us, "When I do this exercise to get a spirit animal, I am disappointed. I think I am making it up; I block my visions and freeze up. I've never had time for animals in my life. In all my memory I can think of only one time when I had any connection with an animal. When I was a teenager, a hawk flew over me when I was hiking. It dove down and narrowly missed my head. I didn't think too much about it. The next day, in another meadow, the hawk returned. It dove down again, and I thought it was going to attack me. I could see its talons and its beak. I wondered if it had a nest nearby and was protecting its young. The next day, I hiked again. This time I went to yet another meadow. The hawk returned and flew over, screeching all the while." The hawk is his spirit animal. Just because the hawk did not come in a guided imagery exercise does not mean it is not his.

The spirit animals are the wisdom keepers of the earth's energy and magic. They know when and how to come to us. When we see out of the eyes of the animals, we hear the wisdom that resonates within them about the earth's energy. We hear how to be in balance and harmony with the earth. We hear how to be one with the earth. That is what they tell us.

How to Hear Your Spirit Animal Speak

How do you hear the voice of the animal? Within the mystical silence, it reverberates in your head. It is the same way you hear music in your mind. It *reverberates.*

How to Hear the Spirit Animals' Voices

When the spirit animal speaks to you, you will feel it as thoughts that are clearer, more focused, and sound slightly different than the ordinary. They may have a new cadence, an accent, a new way of speaking. It is subtle. Ask for the spirit animal or ancient one to speak to you, then listen and pay attention to the thoughts you are having. If your mind wanders, as is natural, bring it back.

Your goal is to be able to receive a clear, coherent message from your spirit animal that has a teaching and a theme that you can remember and use in your life. It takes practice, but it will happen. As you listen to the voices of your spirit animals more and more, you will be able to understand them better as they call to you in the physical world. The messages from your spirit animals come back to you whenever you remember the animal. The animal is a pointer to the message.

As you go through your day, look for animals around you. If you live in a city, you can make this more likely if you go to a place where spirit animals live. Even in the city, however, there are remarkable animal happenings. There are peregrine falcons in New York City; bears in Ocala, Florida, near Disney World; and mountain lions in Los Angeles.

When you see a physical animal, look it in the eye, look at it deeply, look at it sideways. Be attentive to thoughts and feelings you have. Spirit animals will give you thoughts that are unusual, and you will suddenly feel like you are slightly out of space. This is the experience of the animal coming to you. When you see a physical animal behaving in an unusual way, it may be a sign that it is your spirit animal. When that happens, listen carefully.

All animals are our teachers, all can be spirit animals to us. Look deeply in the eyes of an animal. Listen to your thoughts, ask the animal to speak to you, listen to what you are thinking, what it is telling you. Animals talk to us through our thoughts, our bodies, and our emotions. They reach that place below words, surfacing as images we can hold on to.

A woman seeking her spirit animal saw a horse—a beautiful, huge horse that stood above her and looked in her eyes. The next time she did a guided imagery, the horse spoke to her, and she described it like this: "It seemed like a thought in my head, like an inner voice. It sounded different from my voice. It seemed ethereal, grand, definite. Of course, I started to put myself down and tell myself I was making it up, but I knew better. This voice seemed to come from inside me and outside me at once. He said, 'Get on my back! I will take you up into the sky to Her heart.' And I got on the horse's back and he flew upward, higher and higher, and took me to where I could get my visions."

Make it up. Embellish it with imagination. Create, and fill in the blanks. Use your imagination to let your visions and inner voices come to you. You may say to yourself, "I am making this up." Yes, that is the correct feeling. You are creating and receiving images at the same time. That is the feeling of visionary space.

You Need to Quiet Down to Hear the Voices of the Animals

The river speaks: "To hear voices of animals it is essential to quiet down. You need to create a mystical silence away from the material world where you call them and invite them to come." The spirit animals say, "Quiet down, invite us, we will come." Take a walk, paddle on a river, or hike in the mountains to where the animals live. Go to a park. Then let your eyes drift, your ears listen for any sound. When you see a shape, like a cloud, let it form into a spirit. They say, "It is us coming to you. Listen with your inner ear, not to sounds; see with your inner eye, not sights, and we will come to you. There is a pause, a moment of rest, then we will start telling you the story. It will sound like your own thoughts but different. Clearer, more straightforward, like listening to a voice with its own character. It is the inner voice of the living earth speaking through the animals as your own inner voice. When we come to you it is a merging of you and us."

Listen to the stories when they come to you. They can be long. They are clearest as poetry, as a story, as a vision. They will tell you what you are to do in your life. Ask a question. Listen to your animal guide answer. Watch for signs all day. The spirits will appear as the real animal or as a shape or sound, over and over again. The hawk lands on the tree above your head and looks directly into your eyes. The hawk comes and recognizes you.

They say, "You will receive messages and teachings, but they are not always direct. They have been riddles since the beginning of time. In a riddle, there is room for you to enter, for your own voice to fill in and make it relate to your life. Then the communion of us and you happens and it is the world being created. We will tell you what you need to know to grow, and do what you need to do in this lifetime. Because it is from us, it will always be about making the world sacred, saving the animals and the earth, healing and balance. That is the voice you are tapping into. Be specific about which voice you want to hear. That is the one who will answer. If you want a voice of healing, of balance, that is who you will get. Voices of pure greed are not here. Animals speak only in balance. They take what they use, they do not amass wealth."

Create Your Own Stories from the Animals' Voices

You will hear the spirit animals' voices and then create your own stories with your capacity for intuitive wisdom and imagination. Your thoughts will come to you like a creative idea; it can be like a voice, a vision, a thought. If it is a vision, you will see the animals by simply picturing them in your mind. Open yourself to these images. See the owl in a park, where it would be, look up, put it in your mind. It can be in a dream as well or in a waking moment. You can see an owl in your office on the back of your chair. See it fly with you from meeting to meeting. Let the owl be in the room with you. It can be outside the window in a tree. Use your mind's eye.

How to Use the Animals' Voices as an Oracle

Animals speak to you in signs—a feather, a bird flying over you, an owl calls, you see a mountain lion cross the road. The language of animals is silence. People who have pets know this; their pets talk to them as knowledge, as inner thoughts, as emotions. The spirit animals are a doorway to deep intuitive realization. The animals' messages come to you as an intuitive thought.

MARY:

"I saw the panther, and she said, 'It is simple, the animal is about the power of manifestation, the medicine wheel literally brings the animal back.' This thought came to me as though it were a voice, a statement went through my head as if it came from outside of me. I am open to animals saying things, so this is what happens. In another example, I noticed an eagle making spirals high in the sky. I was with my daughter, anxious about her growing up. I realized that eagle is on an air current spiraling high, higher effortlessly; she sees perspectives far greater than mine. She sees way beyond what I can see. I suddenly realize that her message is about effortless dreams, her message to me is to have perspective over a whole lifetime, to see it all, my entire life, to see beyond this obstacle in the moment.

"The eagle was the oracle. I did not even ask a question, yet her voice gave me my answer. If I had taken the eagle stone out of the bag, it would have been the same. Eagle would have told me her story of perspective and power, and it would have given me strength."

The spirit animals communicate to you without words, below words. It is a gut feeling, a feeling in your heart of being one with something, of being moved and touched, of being taken care of and loved. When you put it in words, it says, "I love you; thank you for listening to me; I want to be heard; I want you to help heal yourself, others, and the earth." It reverberates.

How to Listen to the Ancient Ones

In this chapter you will learn to connect with the ancient spirits and guides. These spirits are around you, waiting to communicate with you. They are part of the earth's structure and are instrumental in healing and growing spiritually. In our view, the ancient ones are the memory of the earth. They are accessible to us in the same way that our own memories are. They are the consciousness of the living earth.

First you must open yourself up to the possibility that they exist and are around you. Next, invite them to come to you. Finally, open your eyes and look for them. They are there and they will come to you.

Going to Where the Ancient Ones Lived

The ancient ones were skilled in finding special places that were precious, especially sacred, powerful, and holy places where the resonances were higher and the earth's powers more easy to access. That is where they did ritual and where you can most easily hear their voices, but know that hearing the voices of the ancient ones is not always easy. When we build a whole city over a sacred site it muffles their voices, and they are harder to recognize.

Look for sacred sites in nature, the springs, rivers, mountains, caves, ancient trees. Sometimes we are fortunate enough to find sites where ceremony was done, such as mounds, stone circles, petroglyphs, temple sites, churches, or ley lines. Follow the paths to village sites, places of trade, old routes of travel. Ask yourself, "Is my house built over or near a sacred site?"

To find sacred sites, allow yourself to travel following your own keen sense of knowing. Follow your feeling of being pulled to a particular place. Trust your instinct to go in that direction. Or you can read about sacred sites, search for them on the Internet, and then follow your instincts about which one feels best. Sometimes you will discover that the place you have located is only a parking lot in front of a restaurant but if you pause and look around, you can see what was there before. You might see an entire valley before you, and the ancient ones will appear to you.

Calling Them Forth

When you go visit a sacred site, call the spirits to come to you. Make a medicine wheel. Invite them, out loud or in your thoughts. All you need to do is concentrate and call them forth with intention.

All traditions did this as a prayer or invocation. Most traditions involved a ritual and an offering. Here is a prayer to bring the ancient ones to you.

Great Spirit, come to me in my sacred work. I thank you for the earth and its directions. I thank you for this day with all its beauty. I call the ancient ones to come to me and help me with this sacred work. I invite them to come and tell me what I need to do in my life. I invite them to come to me and tell me who I am and what I am to do. I will go and receive the gifts from the ancient ones and do what I can to heal myself, others, and the earth.

Listen and wait. The ancient ones will come to you. They will speak. It may not be in words or thoughts but rather in dreams, visions, or happenings. The prayer or rituals you choose are up to you. As you become experienced in calling in the spirits, you will discover your own way of doing this. You can also invoke the ancient ones with guided imagery. Guided imagery is a prayer or a meditation that directs your mind to be receptive to certain thoughts. The exercise for meeting your spirit animal in the previous chapter can also be used to meet an ancient one. It will call forth spirit guides as well as spirit animals. What is most important is to be open to the voices coming to you anytime. In any vision, an ancient one can speak to you.

The medicine wheel is one of the most basic ways of calling in the ancient spirits. The ancient ones recognize the medicine wheel and come to you as you build it. The medicine wheel defines sacred space and invites spirits clearly. Act with intent, pray, and open yourself up to their voices.

Michael shares this story of a spirit meeting. "One day I was paddling down the river. It was a beautiful day, but there were no animals around. I looked out of the corner of my eyes keeping a watch out for hawks, otter, bobcats. Suddenly I saw a shape in the woods that caught my eye. I thought it was a man up in a tree, standing tall. He was dressed in a bearskin with the head of the bear pulled over his nose. He was about ten feet up in the tree, moving his head. I paddled over to him for a closer look, he shimmered in the forest and I could not see him clearly. As I watched him, he began to look more and more like a bear shaman, and then he spoke to me. 'Welcome to my river. I am bear shaman, the keeper of this part of the river. I was the ancient shaman of this village. We have been waiting for you; we have come from far away to tell our story. We want our story told. I have a message for you today, a teaching. It is for your book, for your people to know from me. I will have a message for you each day. My message today is: We will speak to you whenever you look for us, whenever you come into our territory and call for us. Whenever you listen, we will speak. Tell your people that if they want to hear my voice, to see the ancient ones, the ancient shamans who once could change into bears, into owls, into mountain lions, into turtles, they have to want to hear us. They have to come and look for us. They have to open their eyes to us, open their ears to us. And then they have to wait and be patient and we will appear.' "

On this path, be patient, do not judge anything. When you see the spirit, it is natural to say "I am making this up. This is really a tree root, a branch. There is nothing there." That is a judgment. Let the spirits come to you. Invite them to come, then accept what you see. Welcome them. If you see an owl in a tree, say, "Thank you, owl spirit, for coming," and then you will see her again. If you say, "There is nothing there," next time you will see nothing. To have your world populated again by spirits, welcome them, recognize them. Invite them, and see them without judgment.

Be patient during this process. When you call them, they may not come immediately. It may be minutes, hours, days, months before they appear. Then all of a sudden you see them. And they are there. There are minutes or hours where nothing much appears to be happening, but these times are punctuated by the most intense moments of visions. Be thankful for the pause. If you were in visions all the time, it would be difficult to live!

Call them and they will come.

WHAT IS THE POWER OF EACH ANIMAL?

THE POWER OF the animal is the true nature of that animal. It is simple. We learn the stories of the animals by looking into their eyes, dreaming about them, honoring them. There are still many animals all around us. We see them in the wild, in zoos, and on TV. You already know a great deal about your spirit animals. You have been watching them for many years. Trust your own knowledge. You do not need to read a book to know about an animal.

Imagine a great eagle, swooping down with talons stretched out, ready to capture its prey. Birds of prey take you. Where they take you is up to them and—sometimes—you. You can be taken into your dreams, into your fear of the darkness, into a world where things are hunted. You may go inside their cries and listen to them speak to each other. You begin to scan the landscape for sound and movement. You become a hunter, a hunter of your own visions, and eventually you find yourself. You go into your darkness, your own nature, and your own life. That is the nature of the eagle power animal, and so it is with the others as well.

A skeptical man came to one of our workshops to please his wife. Much to his surprise, in the workshop he met a coyote. The coyote came to him and looked at him, and while the man was still registering his surprise, the coyote slid into his body. It was a trick—the coyote fooled him into letting him in despite his resistance. Then the coyote said to him from inside his own voice, "Look through my eyes. Keep your sense of humor. You're too serious! Have fun!" The stunned man kept listening as his own voice told him things he had never thought: "It is hard to keep your sense of humor when you are in a battle for survival. I know this. The work you do to support your family is difficult; it takes a toll on you. Do it indirectly, sneak up on it, let it be fun for you, laugh." Once the man thought about it, he realized that the coyote has always been about laughing. They look funny, sly, sneaky, and wild, too. When they call in the night in the distance, they remind us that nature is still alive.

When we teach the Path of the Feather in elementary schools we ask the children, "What is the power of the bear?" They tell us, "The bear is a loner, a great hunter. It is not mean but it is powerful and strong. It is successful in getting food. The bear knew how to live, it had nothing to be afraid of. The bear had much to teach."

What about the turtle? The children say, "The turtle is consistent. It is slow and deliberate. He carries his home and shelter with him. It is close to the ground, to the earth."

What about owl? The children say, "The owls are about the night. The owl sees in the darkness. It can catch its prey, move quickly, perch high. It can watch from above. It is about wisdom."

Ask Yourself What the Animal Means to You

To ask yourself what any animal means to you, relax deeply, close your eyes and rest a moment. Ask for the animal's voice to come to you. Ask the animal to tell you who it is.

See the animal in your mind's eye. Watch it move, walk in its footprints. Follow it along its journey. It may glance at you. If it does, look directly in its eyes. Now imagine seeing out of its eyes. Feel its body and the way it moves, feel its balance and its grace. Feel the ground under its feet, look around you. See what it pays attention to. Flow into the animal's way of being. Feel your own being transformed into the animal's.

Now open your eyes and write the first things about the animal that come to mind. Perhaps you can go see your animal in the wild, in a zoo, or on TV and then write down your impressions. The more you see your animal, the more you learn about its power and spirit. After its body speaks, its spirit will sing to you in shamanic songs and visions. They begin to speak louder, they talk in poems and images, and they tell you who they are in the spirit world. They are speaking to you as your spirit guide.

Take note of the animals that live near you. Every place has its animals. In New York State, it is the bear, hawk, owl, dove. Florida has alligators, snakes, dolphins, deer. Remember the animals that were there but are now gone, like the buffalo. Remember the prehistoric animals, the mastodon, the saber-toothed tiger. And remember the animals that are endangered, like the Florida panther. These animals will populate your own medicine wheel. Call forth the animals; listen for their calls; hear the hawk, the owl, the crow. See their footprints. Walk in their footprints.

An All-Day Exercise for Looking out of the Eyes of Your Animal

The ancient ones speak to us: "We are telling you about a ritual. You can only see what your animal can see."

To perform this exercise, go to a sacred place near your house. It can be within a couple of hours' drive or nearer. Pick the place that is the most sacred to you, that resonates within your soul.

Before you leave, choose a spirit animal to be with you on this special day. You will look out of the eyes of this animal, so choose the animal that you want to be your teacher. If you have a spirit animal that you are working with or that you have chosen to be in your medicine wheel, you can choose that animal.

In this special ritual, you can only see what your animal can see. You can only go where your animal can go. All day, during this sacred ritual, you will be the animal. If you have chosen a bear, repeat over and over again as you drive, as you walk, "I can only see what the bear can see, I can only go where the bear can go." It is like a mantra, a refrain, a chant. Look at your landscape through the bear's eyes.

You can do this in the present or in the distant past if the animal no longer lives in the place where you are. Imagine the landscape as it once was, or you can leave it the way it is. You have plenty of time, so you can look out of the animal's eyes in the present and in many different times.

Now listen for the voice of your animal or even the voice of the animal shaman. They will speak to you and tell you their stories. This is when they will be at their strongest. Remember you have plenty of time. You can do your meditation all day or as long as you wish.

When you reach your destination, act like the animal. Run, play, and as you do, they will speak to you. When you walk, imagine that you leave the footprints of the animal. Let them speak to you and guide your movements. They will direct the ritual if you let them.

Throughout the meditation, chant "I can only see what the animal can see." If you wish, you can smell and feel as the animal. Feel the breeze and breathe in the smell of the rich earth. Remember, this is a sacred exercise to perform all day. If you want to, put on an animal costume; even one feather or representative object helps. The shaman of old would wear a complete bearskin and mask, and that is how she saw out of the eyes of the bear.

You can see out of their eyes as a shaman animal, as an animal lover, or as a visionary animal. Listen carefully and see if your animal will sing a song to you or speak to you in an inner voice. Listen for the ancient shamans. They may tell you to perform a certain ritual or to do something to save that animal. They may give you prayers or chants, or tell you what they did as the animal shaman. You can see only what your animal can see.

Guided Imagery for Your Spirit Animal

This exercise lets you experience seeing out of the eyes of your spirit animal using guided imagery. *Close your eyes, make yourself comfortable. If you wish, uncross your legs, allowing your body to relax deeply. Feel your body supported by your chair as you let go of tension. Now let your breathing slow and become deeper. Feel your abdomen rise and fall as you slowly breathe in and out.*

Now let your feet relax. Feel the wonderful sense of relaxation spread upward to your legs. You may feel heaviness or tingling as you relax. If you do, enjoy those feelings and let them deepen and spread. Now let your legs relax. Feel the muscles lengthen as you relax more deeply. Let your pelvis relax, your belly relax, your chest relax. Let the feelings spread to your arms and hands. Now let your neck and face relax, let your jaw drop, let your eyes relax by seeing a horizon and blackness. Let the top of your head relax. Let your whole body relax deeply.

Now imagine you are on a sacred river. This river is very special. It flows from sacred springs. It flows crystal clear, from the beginning of time to the end of time. Now let yourself float out of the headwaters and drift down the river. You can be on a raft, on a canoe or kayak, or you can float on the water itself. The water is warm. It carries you and you are perfectly safe. See yourself being taken by the river. Feel yourself on the river being taken by its flow. Feel the water caressing your body. If you are on a raft, let your hands go over the side and touch the water. Feel the water flowing in an easy, gentle, caressing way; feel the water supporting you. If you wish, you can be submerged in the river. See yourself diving, rising, playing in the water.

Look upward. See the trees dappled in sunshine; see them glimmer and shimmer in the reflected moving light from the river. In the trees, you can see the ancient spirits. They stand by the sacred river and hold the place. Let yourself relax yet more deeply as you move downriver. You are immersed in a deep feeling of comfort, you are embraced by sacred waters of the earth. Feel the water touch you as though you are embraced by Her love.

Now see an otter on the bank of the river. See her diving and rising near the tree roots. Notice her beautiful black shiny coat. See how she moves. She is so graceful; she is in perfect harmony with the water and her environment. It seems as if she is one with the river, as if her beautiful black coat is part of the river, her diving at one with the river's movement. She moves with such ease. Now allow yourself to see out of the eyes of the otter. Open your inner eyes as the otter and see what she sees. Notice the bottom of the river, the pebbles, the river grasses flowing gracefully and gently in the water. See the fish, the changing bottom textures. Now feel yourself in the otter's body. Be an otter.

Feel yourself play, twirl, dive, and rise. Come up under a log, dive again under the surface. All your moves are graceful. As an otter, you are one with the river, flowing as the river flows.

Now come up and return to your own body. Rest for a moment on the riverbank. You can feel the sun on your face, kissing you. You are embraced by the love and the beauty of the earth. Now look up. In a tree on the side of the river you see an owl. The owl stares into your eyes. You can feel yourself being taken by the owl. Allow yourself to be taken. Go into the owl's soft gray feathers. Go into the owl's body. Turn around inside her. Now you are the owl. You can see out of the eyes of the owl. You can see the sun. Open your inner owl eyes, eyes that have clarity. Every detail is sharp and crisp. You are at ease in this powerful body. You fear nothing. You are silent and still, and you can be this way for hours.

Feel your body covered with feathers. They are beautiful, soft, and colored with brown and yellow stripes. You are elegant and powerful. Now turn your head around. You can turn it virtually all the way around and see on all sides. Feel the power of your wings beating the air for takeoff. Feel yourself gracefully fly. Your wings are expansive. They are five feet across. Your body is large, and you use your power effortlessly. Gracefully and silently you fly. Now look back, see the river below you as if you were an owl.

Now leave the owl and return to your own body sitting by the river. You feel totally at ease in your own body. You now have the gracefulness of the otter, the clarity of seeing like the owl. You are transformed. You will never be the same again. Now the river is your home. The water, the sun, the trees are your home. You are embraced by the earth, you are at ease. Now you realize how beautiful you are. Let the river take you and carry this feeling of ease with you all day.

You can create this imagery for any animal. What you will see is the story of the animal for your own personal vision quest.

About Animal Transformations

In ancient times, the shaman would transform into an animal. Anthropologists call this phenomenon a human-animal transformation. In his visions, the shaman would become an animal, flying as an owl, or dancing as a bear. The shaman then portrayed the experience as art to share with his people.

One goal of the medicine wheel and all its animals is to help you experience a human-animal transformation. In the center of the medicine wheel, your spirit animal takes you in human form. The medicine wheel creates sacred space in which you can become an animal again. In human-animal transformation, you transcend ordinary time and space. You are in harmony, woven into the fabric of earth, like the animal.

As a human-animal transformation, you acquire the power of the animal more deeply. We begin by seeing out of the owl's eyes, but quickly progress to becoming the owl. The medicine wheel is all around you, and you are now part of the sacred mystery. The owl can speak to you and speak through you to others.

Making a medicine wheel and seeing out of the eyes of the animals is the practice required to bring about human-animal transformation. By performing the ritual over and over again, you bring the animals to you. Each time you see out of the eyes of an animal you move deeper and deeper into the experience of the shaman.

The Directions of the Compass

The Directions

The four directions have been sacred throughout human history. Each has its element, its correspondence to the position of the sun, its energy, and its spiritual meaning. The elements are air, fire, water, and earth. The sun positions are sunrise, noon, sunset, and night. The energies are beginning, present, ending, and the unformed. The meanings are change, manifestation, healing, and grounding. More than just mere compass points, the directions are forces that organize the spirit world. When you make a medicine wheel, the meanings of the directions are crucial to understanding the wheel's message. The directions give the medicine wheel its story; they are the coherent orientation of spiritual space.

Each people had its own interpretation of the meaning of the directions. The ones we give here were given to us by our spirit animals and ancient ones. In time, when you have worked with medicine wheels, you will learn your own meanings of the directions. The meanings will be somewhat different for each situation and for that specific medicine wheel.

East

East is the air (wind), sunrise, the beginning, and change. East is the hope for the future, anticipation, the birth of new things, the dawn of a new day, the glimmer of the first light. East is how your life will change as you grow and become a shaman.

East is new beginnings and change.

South

South is fire, high noon, the present, passion, and manifestation. South is embodied energy, love, the fullness of the day. South is your outer life, what you are actually involved in now, what is seen in the brightness of the day, what we bring forth of ourselves, our presentation. South is falling in love and manifesting what we want.

South is the present and manifestation.

West

West is water, sunset, completion, and healing. West is about inner spaces, renewal, endings, and letting go. West is your inner life; it is deep dreams and having faith. West is where your images come from, where healing power comes from.

West is endings and healing.

North

North is earth, night, the void, and grounding. North is family, work, the cornerstone. North holds you safe. North is about protection, the night energies, the vast spaciousness of the void in the universe. North is the magnetic forces of the earth, the unknown, the unformed. North takes visions and sends them into the collective consciousness and then everywhere in the universe.

North is the unformed and grounding.

Center

The center is the essence, the Creator, God, the Goddess, you. Center is who you are, who She is, the Mother, our Source, the energy that we want to balance and heal the earth. Center is our intention, our being, our power.

Center is essence.

Intermediate Directions

The intermediate directions—the southeast, the southwest, the northwest, and the northeast—create balance in the circle by holding space. They make the space they are in sacred simply by being there. Holding space means resting in balance and harmony. These directions are the guardians. When an animal is in an intermediate direction, directions on each side of it are balanced and the medicine wheel remains completely populated at all times. When the medicine wheel is populated, it is full of the rich sacred energy of all the spirit animals.

The Medicine Wheel for Sacred Space

SACRED SPACE IS about meaning. When a stone is in the road, it can be just an impediment. If, however, the stone were the place where a revered religious leader sat, it would be sacred. If the stone were the place the leader died or was reborn, it would be so sacred that millions of people would make a pilgrimage to it each year from all over the earth. Space is made sacred by the story you believe in.

In the Path of the Feather, all space is sacred, and eventually you will see that no place is more sacred than another. Sacred space requires a shift in consciousness, from seeing wherever you are as ordinary to seeing it as holy. In the Path of the Feather, the shift is up to you, and the medicine wheel is the tool you use to sanctify the space around you.

The medicine wheel makes space sacred by bringing in the energies of all the directions and all the spirit animals. Perhaps more accurately, it is your intention to honor those energies that sanctify. This technique of creating sacred space is very ancient, possibly the most ancient way of all. All you need to do is act—place the animals, and sacred space will be created for you in your life now. As you learn what the animals represent, the space will grow in meaning.

Placing objects of importance to you within your circle further personalizes the space and makes it a refuge. Jewelry, presents from people you love, found stones, found feathers—all these make the medicine wheel more beautiful.

Sacred space is a recognition of the balance among the different directions. A balance of change, passion, healing, and grounding, of air, fire, water, and earth. Your animals bring this energy into your own life through the doorway of the medicine wheel. Listen to them speak.

Medicine Wheel One: A Medicine Wheel for Sacred Space

The time has come to act on your sacred impulse, to create a sacred space.

Close your eyes and say,

I call forth
The spirit animals of the medicine wheel.
I call forth

The ancient ones
And the powers of the wheel
To create sacred earth.

- State your intention to create sacred space in a prayer. Either follow this invocation, or pray the way you usually do. It may be verbally, out loud, silently to yourself, a repeated prayer, a mantra, you could close your eyes, or go into a trance. You can't do this wrong; it is simple; even silence is right.

May this medicine wheel make my space sacred; may it call in the spirit animals; may it bring peace and balance and harmony to the earth. I pray that this space will be holy and full of the healing energy of the earth.

- Orient your map so that the N on the compass faces the picture of the earth on the map. For this medicine wheel, take the stones out of the bag one at a time without seeing them. Reach in the bag, take out a stone, and place it, then pick the next one. Reach in and pick the stones by chance. Each spirit animal is sacred, and sacred space will be created. As you make more medicine wheels and get to know the animals better, choose your own animal and place it with intent. The wheel will become your own as you choose the animals that are sacred to you and that speak to you.

When we make medicine wheels, we pick up the animal stones and put them down in the directions one by one. As we place the stones, we move into sacred space—we go into a trance and an altered state. From this sacred space, we place the stone and pray for what we want to know or what we want to happen. That is it. The process is simple; the medicine wheel is a living prayer, a manifestation of our being, love, belief, and embodiment.

Now, reach into the bag and take out the first stone. Place the first stone faceup in the center of the map. "Oh holy one, oh holy earth, I call forth the power of the center, the cornerstone of my own essence. As I place my stone in the center, I become the central axis around which the world spins." This stone, the essence stone, represents you. The animal on this stone is the dimension or the side of you that will be sanctified in this wheel. It is the part of you that will be healed. In placing this stone, you put yourself in the center of the medicine wheel, in alignment with an axis of the earth. As you place this stone, pause and make your connection with the living earth.

Reach in the bag and take out the next stone. Place this animal in the east, the direction of the sunrise. "O holy one, o holy earth, I call forth the power of the east, the cornerstone of the dawn. As I place my stone in the east, I align myself with the energies of a new beginning."

Reach in the bag and take out the next stone. Place this animal in the south, the direction of brightest light. "O holy one, o holy earth, I call forth the power of the south, the cornerstone of the midday sun. As I place my stone in the south, I align myself with the energies of actualization, manifestation, and my greatest passion.

Take out another stone. Place this animal in the west, the direction of the dusk and the setting sun. "O holy one, o holy earth, I call forth the power of the west, the cornerstone of the great waters. As I place my stone in the west, I align myself with the energies of faith, of letting go, and of my dreams."

Take out the final stone and place it in the north, the direction of the earth power. "O holy one, o holy earth, I call forth the power of the north, the cornerstone of the void. As I place my stone in the north, I align myself with the energies of the universe, the spinning of the earth on its axis, the movement and the mystery of life."

Look at the animals who have come to greet you in sacred space. They are the power animals that will orient you to the directions. With their arrival comes the energies of the east, the south, the west, and the north.

Next comes the outer ring. The animals that dwell here are the guardian spirits of your wheel. They protect your sacred self, standing guard over your sacred space.

To make the outer ring, reach into the bag, take out the stones, and place them one at a time, face up. Place a stone in the east, then the south, then the west, and finally the north. Next, place stones between these stones in the southeast, the southwest, the northwest, and the northeast. You have made an outer circle of eight stones. You have made the basic medicine wheel shape of thirteen stones in three circles (see illustration).

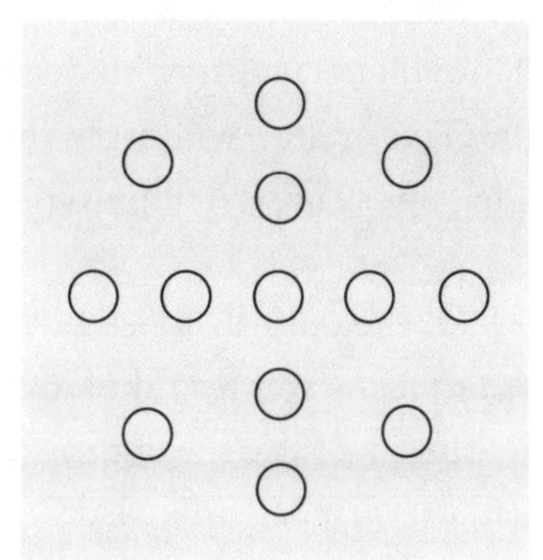

To find out how the spirit animals that have come to you have created sacred space, read the stories about the animals at the back of the book.

First, read the story of the animal you placed in the center of your medicine wheel for sacred space. This animal is the essence stone. It tells you about your place in sacred space. This stone defines the energy of this sacred medicine wheel.

- Now read the story of the animal you placed in the east. This animal tells you how you can begin to create sacred space in your life. This animal gives you the way to start.
- Now read the story of the animal you placed in the south. This animal tells you how to create sacred space in your greatest illumination. It tells you how to put passion and love into sacred space and how to make the space manifest.
- Now read the story of the animal you placed in the west. This animal will tell you how you can make sacred space from dreams. It will tell you about what needs to be healed so that the space around you will be more sacred.
- Finally, read the story of the animal you placed in the north. This will tell you how to deeply ground the sacred space in your life. This animal will carry the medicine wheel to the void and back out again, full of power.

All the animals together make up a large spinning story like your life. As you read the story of each animal, use your intuition to interpret how the animal speaks to you personally. In the next days, remember animal dreams and listen to the voice of the animal.

You have made your medicine wheel. Your sacred space is complete. The power animals will tell you the stories of how to enhance sacred space in your life. These animals are the teachers called in to create sacred space for you. They are the animals closest to your heart. For example, after you place your animal in the east, it says to you, "This is the beginning, there is change in the wind and the air. The sun rises in the east. I come to you to tell you of the beginning of creating sacred space within, and about change in your life." If your animal is bear, bear might say, "For you to create sacred space, you can look at healing what needs to be healed in your life. Make your life more sacred by healing that now." As you read the animals' stories, ask yourself, "What do I need to do to create sacred space? What problems do I have that keep me from the sacred space I know is around me?" When you read the animal in the east, ask yourself, "How can the energy of east—of beginning and change—combined with that animal's story, create sacred space in my life?" The animal will bring you the answer.

MICHAEL:

"Since I started making medicine wheels, my whole life has changed. I make medicine wheels because I believe they change my reality. They create a sacred space for me in which to live, to work, to lecture, and to do ritual. In my home I have medicine wheels in many places. I have one in my bedroom on my dresser, another on a large table, one on a fireplace I don't light in summer, and another on top of a chest of drawers. I make larger ones at each corner of the house and the largest of all on the property lines with huge redwood sculptures.

"Medicine wheels make wherever I am my sacred home. In a hotel, the room becomes my home the second the medicine wheel is built. I am grounded there, it is now my place on earth. I make wheels on sacred sites I visit, and for every ritual I do. Now I make one at the start of every lecture I give. The exercise makes the room sacred, my lecture sacred."

MARY:

"I made my first medicine wheel in my home. I brought out my Zuni animal fetish carvings and set them up on a table, placing them in the four directions with the help of a compass. I looked out of the windows at the landscape in each direction and noted the location of the river and the prairies. I looked out and imagined the animals that were around. With this medicine wheel, my house became my sacred home.

"When I made this medicine wheel, I saw that in Florida where I live, the panther lived in the south, the bear in the west, the turtle in the north, the owl in the east. Specifically for me, an owl lived in my backyard to the east of my house. The turtles lived in the river that was to the north. The Florida panther lived in the Big Cypress Swamp in the Everglades far to the south of my house. The Florida bear lived in the Suwanne Wildlife Preserve near Cedar Key to the west.

"After I created the medicine wheel, I felt grounded. I knew where I was and I felt a sense of being deeply connected with the earth. I felt as though I were one within the earth."

Finding the Animals Around You

After you've made this first medicine wheel several times, you can begin to experiment with how you choose the animals that inhabit it. One way of enhancing the sacredness and increasing the relevance of the wheel is to attune it to the environment around you.

Ask yourself what animals live around you and where they dwell. Touch each stone, either on the wheel or in the medicine bag, and ask yourself where that animal you placed lives in relation to your home. For example, as you touch the owl in its direction, you ask, "Are there owls in there? Can I see with my mind's eye the trees that are their homes?" As you pull a bear from your medicine bag, ask, "Where do bears live in my landscape?" Don't restrict yourself to thinking about only where the animals live now. Consider where they might have lived in the past. After all, this medicine wheel invites the spirit animals—those that have always been—into your life. Even if the animal has moved on, the spirit still dwells there. Even in Manhattan there once were bears, deer, and mountain lions. There are still bears in large numbers to the north of Manhattan in the Adirondack Mountains.

A young law student was confused about which path to follow in life. Although she felt confident of her interest in the law, life as a corporate attorney did not have the same appeal to her that it did to her friends. Seeking guidance, the young woman attended a Path of the Feather workshop. In her mind's eye, she saw a cat. *No surprise,* she thought. *I have several cats at home, and I'm probably just thinking of them.* The next day, however, as she walked to campus, she saw a billboard that caught her attention. On it was a cougar looking out at her. She realized that she had been visited the previous night not by an ordinary house cat but by a sleek cougar. That night she made a medicine wheel to get a message from her cougar. The cougar spoke to her: "I am endangered. I am your spirit animal. When I came to you, I came to ask you a favor. You need to protect the cougar. By inviting me into your medicine wheel, you acquired responsibility. It is a bargain. I will give you my power to fight in court. You, in return, will save us." Now she knew what to do. She became the legal representative for an organization that fought to save the cougar in her state. She filed a lawsuit to protect and acquire habitats the cougar needed to survive.

Move the animals around and place them where you want them to be, where they have told you to place them or where they live in reality. Your medicine wheel deepens your reality of being with the animal in the physical world and in the spirit world. It will grow in power as the sacred landscape around you encompasses your sacred wheel. It spins from the little wheel you are making in your personal space to the world around you.

This medicine wheel is an act of great beauty and power. However you place your animals—either without looking at them or later where you know they live—sacred space will be formed around you and those you love. Sacred space is not trivial. Just the existence of sacred space will begin to change your consciousness and change your life.

At this point, you do not need to ask any questions. Simply make the wheel and watch your life change. As you carry on your normal daily activities, you and the world around you will change. Just knowing that you walk around in a vortex of sacred space will make your ordinary life happenings sacred. When you are so attuned, the spirit animals will tell you what you need to do to be on the shamanic path.

Welcome to the shaman's world. You have called in the spirit animals and created a doorway. You have transformed your life into a shamanic journey with the spirit animals that are now with you. This wheel is the first story and the beginning of your teaching. As you make many medicine wheels for sacred space, each animal will stake out its place on your own personal medicine wheel. Each wheel is a teaching, and each will teach you more. You will soon hear your own personal story of where each animal lives and why it has chosen that spot. If the owl takes on a meaning for you of inward seeing and change, you can put her in the east, the place of change. If owl lives to the east of your home, she might be placed in the east in your medicine wheel. The animals can stay in one place or move with time as your story changes. Some of our animals have stayed in one place for years, others move all the time. Sometimes an animal will move for one wheel, and then go back. It is surprising, fun, and creative.

The Vision Quest Oracle

These shaman animals' voices are powerful and strong. They are the wisdom keepers—they walk inside the dreams and physical realms of your own life. As spirit animals, they are in both worlds at once. Animals that live in your life and appear to you are your guardians and teachers. Who better than they to tell you of what is to come for you?

To find guidance, to hear the oracular voice of the Path of the Feather, you must embark on a vision quest. In fact, the oracle itself is a vision quest. Quest and question are related. You ask a question, and the answer comes through a vision. The making of the medicine wheel is the appearance of the vision in the world. It is brought to you by the animal, the guides coming to you as leaders, wisdom keepers, storytellers. The very act of asking, in other words, manifests your answer.

In ancient times, when an initiate went into the wilderness, he took with him his favorite animals in his imagination. If his favorite animal was the wolf, wolf went with him. Wolf, however, led him to the mountaintop to meet lizard. She told him about being ancient and surviving. He went to the east to meet buffalo. Buffalo said, "I will teach you about abundance and spirit." In the south, wolf took him to meet mountain lion: "I will teach you to hunt," lion told him, "about waiting and pouncing." The Path of the Feather will lead you, the modern-day initiate, to meet the animals who have an answer for you.

The medicine wheel will take you on your vision quest, and the animals will come to you as the oracle. Honor the mystery and magic of placing the stones. Put your hand in the bag and let the stone place itself. Let an animal come to you as you go in each direction.

Put yourself in the center. The animals in the four directions are the animal shamans—the voices of your quest. They will speak to you and teach you. Be open, for you go on the vision quest protected by the circle of eight outer animals. You go to the north, take a stone, place it in the medicine wheel. You create an actuality; an animal comes to you in the vision quest. It speaks to you and teaches you.

Medicine Wheel Two: A Medicine Wheel for the Vision Quest Oracle

Orient your compass to the north and spin your map beneath it. Come to rest with the picture of the earth pointing in the same direction as the needle of the compass. Now comes the time to frame the question you want to ask. What do you want the animals to tell you about? Is it who you are? Is it what you are to do in your life? Is it something smaller, more mundane, or is it a larger unformed wondering about the future? Is it specific or general? Is it a fundamental issue or a transient concern? No matter the nature of your question, it is valid. The more clearly you frame your quest, the more meaningful the message from the animals will be.

Framing your question is not difficult. We all know what our own issues are and we know what is on our minds. Deciding what to ask, however, may be difficult. But ask without worry, for you cannot wear out your welcome here. Simply ask the question over and over again as you take the stones out of the bag and place them in the directions. For example, "Tell me about my business?" Then reach in the medicine bag and take out a stone. Pick the stones from the bag without looking at the figures.

- Pick up a stone. Place it facedown in the center of the medicine wheel without looking at what it is. An animal will come to you. Know that you will meet an animal that will accompany you on your vision quest. This animal responds to the essence of your question. This animal will lead you to the answer.
- Pick up a stone. Place it facedown in the north. An animal will come to you. Know that you will meet an animal in the north, in the void. This animal will be the messenger of the vision, the animal that carries the response from the mystery of the unknown.
- Pick up a stone. Place it facedown in the east. An animal will come to you. Know that you will meet the animal in the east as

the sun is rising. This animal will teach you about changes and new beginnings, telling you how your life will be transformed.

~ Pick up a stone. Place it facedown in the south. An animal will come to you. Know that you will meet an animal in the south as the sun is high, and this animal will illuminate the vision of the manifestation. This animal will teach you about actualization, about what will happen out in the world, what will come to its fullness.

~ Pick up a stone. Place it facedown in the west. An animal will come to you. Know that you will meet an animal in the west at sunset. This animal will tell you of your dreams, of what is letting go, of having faith in what is ending.

As you take out stones from the bag and place them one at a time in each direction, the medicine wheel completes its first cycle. You have made an inner circle of four stones around a center stone.

~ Place your next stone in the north outside of the first one and then in the east, the south, and the west, outside the stones you placed in the first circle.

~ Then place the stones in between in the northeast, the southeast, the northwest, and the southwest (see illustration). This wheel has completed its second cycle.

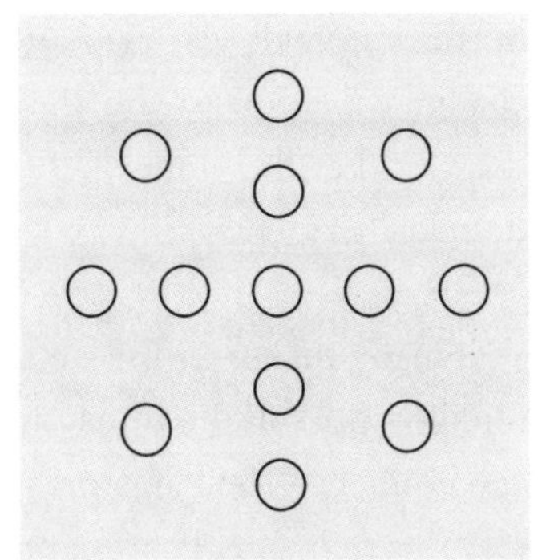

~ Ask your question one last time and turn over the stone in the center. Read the story of that animal. This is the essence of your question. This is the hand that will guide you to the answer.

~ Next comes the north. Turn over this stone, and read the story of the animal in the chapter on each animal. This is the message from the void, from the unknown.

~ On to the east. Turn over this stone, and read the story of the animal. This is the dawn, the story of change, and a glimpse of what will be transformed.

~ Now for the south. Turn over the stone, and read the story of the animal. Here you will find the greatest illumination, the most direct viewing when the shadows are shortest. This will tell you what will be in the world of the senses.

~ Finally, the west. Turn over this stone, and read the story of the animal. This will tell you of your dreams, of what is coming to a close, and what you will have to relinquish.

This is the first answer to your question, the first spiral, the first vision quest journey, the first pilgrimage.

~ Then, turn over the stones in the north, east, south, and west of the outer circle. Read each story as the animal reveals itself. In the north, you will learn about grounding. In the east, lessons of change will come to you. In the south come feelings of passion. In the west lies the language of dreams. These animals are the wisdom keepers. They tell you where the power lies in regard to your question.

~ Finally, turn over the stones between the main directions. The middle stones in the outer circle are the bridge stones that merge and connect. When an animal is a bridge animal it joins the energies on each side. For example, an animal in the southeast joins change in the east, with passion in the south. Read these stories and listen.

The "Instant Oracle"

You may make an "instant oracle" medicine wheel for questions of less complexity and answers with less depth. Do this to spot-check your feelings or inclinations; do this to catch a glimpse of what is to come; do this to spark your thought process.

Begin as you did for the full oracle, orienting your map, asking your question, and placing your stones. This time, you will only place the center stone and one at each direction. Turn over the animals one by one—center, north, east, south, west—and read their stories. These animals will guide you to a less nuanced version of your answer.

Letting Your Intuitive Powers Grow

As you travel along the path, you will come to know the animals so well that when you place the stones you will know what they mean. Using the stones as an oracle is about letting your intuitive power increase and grow. When you know the animals well and you take the bear out of the bag and place it in the center, you know enough about bear to say, "The bear is in the place of my essence, it has to do with healing in my life, with a solitary journey, it has to do with gathering, with hibernation." By knowing the animal's nature, you can instantly see the parts of its story that apply to your question.

Let's say your question is about starting a business. First you put a stone in the center. It is the place of essence, and there you meet lion. She says, "Starting your business requires bravery and power." With this message, you travel north, to see the bear. You know the bear, and you hear it say, "I am bear, I am about healing and responsibility. This is what comes to you from the void. In starting your business, don't forget about healing, don't abandon your responsibility." Then you go to the east and see owl. Owl says, "In the beginning you need insight. Before you start your business look within yourself. Be certain you are ready to meet the challenges ahead of you." Next is south, and there you see the buffalo. Buffalo says, "I am the buffalo, I am about great abundance, and this is what will actualize in your life."

When you take your own personal life issue and put it in the center of sacred space, it becomes the vision quest. Then the shamanic way of being will teach you your path.

We made a medicine wheel as an oracle to tell us about *The Path of the Feather* as we were writing it. We chose the question, "Tell us about *The Path of the Feather*" for the subject of the medicine wheel. With our book as the orientation, the animals spoke to us. To build this medicine wheel, we took the animals out of the medicine bag without looking at them and put them down in the four directions in the order they came out.

In the center, the intention of the question, "Tell us about *The*

Path of the Feather," the serpent came to us; she said, "Shed your old skin and transform into a shaman."

In the darkness of the north, far up in the deepest night, from the mystery, the response came. The owl said to us, "Remember the owl's spirit to bring you deeper into your dreams. Tell your readers never to forget their deepest dreams."

In the east, the beginning, the sunrise, the coyote came to us. For this medicine wheel the coyote said, "Make it playful, make it fun. Do the medicine wheel as if you were coyote. Do it as one with me, as a trickster. Tell the readers to make their medicine wheels in playfulness."

In the south, the place of the full sun at noon, of manifestation, the female bear said, "Give birth to all projects, protect and care for your book as your baby, feed the project. Tell your readers to nurture their work too."

In the west, the eagle said, "I am in daylight to take you to your dream space. See with perspective. I am telling you to see clearly, from up on high, way up on my spiral. Tell your readers to see the whole medicine wheel, to be observant, with keen awareness and sight like an eagle."

Together, all the animals make a story. Each story is different depending on the situation and the person. Our animals tell their stories based on who they are to us. For us, the coyote is trickster, the owl sees in the night. Your animals will tell you the story you need to hear.

So the answer to our question of intent in writing *The Path of the Feather* came in the form of this story: the Path of the Feather is about the transformation of consciousness. Never give up your deepest dreams, make your medicine wheels in playfulness, then nurture them with care. See the whole picture. This was the spirit animals gift to us and to you. This is an example of a medicine wheel created as an oracle.

The medicine wheel is a cycle, a circular story, but it will vary depending on your intention in making it and what significance you give to the directions. The directions are like modifiers and they give the story structure.

An Oracle for Daily Life

A man listened to his wife. She was crying. She told him that she was tired, that she gave all day to her children, her job, her friends, and that she needed a change in her life. She said she was getting sick; her life was too much for her. He did not know what to do. He felt helpless and even frightened, concerned that his family would dissolve before his eyes. He went into the sacred corner of his home office and made a medicine wheel oracle. What could he do, he asked of the medicine wheel, to help his relationship with his wife? The first animal that came to him was a buffalo. He placed the buffalo in the center and recalled that the buffalo is about nurturing. "I feed the whole world; I bring spirituality to my people," buffalo says. He closed his eyes. He saw his wife feeding the family, and he knew he had to nurture her now. He saw that she brought him his spiritual visions in her beauty. He knew he had to value her as precious, and listen to her. She had been buffalo all alone for the family. It was his turn to lighten her burden. When he saw her, he told her what the medicine wheel oracle had told him. He told her he would try his best to nurture her.

The medicine wheel does not just answer a question, it also helps you bring about change in your life. This change is an ongoing process, alive and tied to the earth. For example, when you are called by the bear stone, the bear energy enters your life. Your consciousness of the bear deepens. You will begin to see bears all around you. You find bear stories in the newspapers.

Then your life starts to change. By asking your question, you unleash the shamanic powers within you and of the earth. You may, for example, start to have bear dreams and visions. If you are interested in healing, in making things right, your bear healer emerges. If you are concerned about your family, your bear protector emerges. If you have to do something that you are afraid of, your bear courage emerges. Just as the spirit animals tell you the answer you seek, they also give you the means to make their prediction real.

The Medicine Wheel for Manifestation

Manifesting Your Dreams

The medicine wheel can also manifest your desires and dreams. Once you have created sacred space and found the answers you seek, once you know who you are and your purpose, the next step is to manifest that vision on earth. You do not need to know what you want precisely. You only need to be on the sacred path. The medicine wheel will take your visions, put them in sacred space, and balance them with the earth and manifest them within Her body. When we use the medicine wheel for manifestation, it becomes a prayer in harmony with the earth and Her vision becomes manifest through you.

That which you wish to manifest need not be physical. You

can wish to manifest a proper direction in life, perhaps a feeling of contentment, perhaps just a direction to follow.

The medicine wheel is a powerful tool to make your dreams come true. Drawing upon the energies of the earth, it recasts your dreams and desires in a healing light, restructuring them in harmony.

This medicine wheel is a ceremony to manifest change in your life. It infuses the spirit inside your own journey. In this medicine wheel, the center stone is the animal you become. The center stone is your power animal.

In a medicine wheel for manifestation, you call forth an animal to be with you and give you power. If you are a lawyer in court, a parent, a physician, a person starting a new business, you call the animal to give you the power of its nature. This cultivation of a relationship with a power animal can last a day, a month, or years. You will meet new animals along the way. While we had owls for years, the snakes came one day, then the bears. You can have many animals at once or individual ones sequentially.

Mary manifested the Arts in Medicine program at Shands, University of Florida. This world-renowned program brings artists into the hospital to work with patients, changing the atmosphere of the whole hospital. Mary used medicine wheels to harness her vision and allow it to manifest as greater than her own. Her medicine wheel changes each day. One day, she placed beaver in the center for building and creating. She placed turtle in the east to ground the program from the start, lion in the south for power of manifestation, bear in the west for the power of healing art, and buffalo in the north for abundance and funding the program and artists. She prays for the needs of the program to be met and for her vision to manifest on earth. She prays in each direction for the program to be full, for growth, for sacredness, and for healing.

The program started with one artist in residence in the bone marrow transplant unit, but now, seven years later, over four hundred artists have worked with patients. Mary has begun implementing programs all over the state of Florida. Her own vision became her quest to manifest a creative arts program, which has become her shamanic path.

Seeking to manifest healing in life or wishing for deliverance from suffering, or praying for the good health of all—these are steps beyond listening to the spirit animals, beyond consulting them. Manifestation is in the realm of sophisticated shamanism. It seeks the loan of the powers of the spirit world to make reality in the real world.

Earlier, you sought the answer to a question. At this moment the oracle is fulfilled, the *intention* of your world and the spirit world are joined. Your wish, however, must be in harmony with the wishes of those whose power you will borrow. You wish to heal, the animals wish to be heard—it is a symbiotic relationship. However, if you wish to churn, to build, to tear down, the manifestation cannot proceed.

Medicine Wheel Three: A Medicine Wheel for Manifestation

Orient your compass to the north and spin the map beneath it until it faces the picture of the earth. Take the stones out of your bag and lay them faceup in front of you; for this medicine wheel, you will choose which animal goes in each direction.

However, to do this you need to know something about each animal and about the directions. You are choosing to manifest something, and you should make your decision carefully. Do you wish to manifest something that begins with rebirth? Then place snake in the east. Do you wish passion to be the underpinning of this reality? Then lion belongs in the north. Calling in the spirit animals for manifestation is a shamanic creative act, your first one on the Path of the Feather.

If you have not read the stories or don't feel comfortable yet placing the animals faceup with intent, you can take the stones out of the bag and put them down without looking at them, as you did with the first and second medicine wheels. As you grow to know your spirit guides, you will learn how to place animals by choice.

In this medicine wheel, you will create three spirals, each one taking you deeper into your vision. The first wooden stone describes your intention, the next ring allows you to see out of the eyes of the animals, and the last ring makes it manifest in the spirit world.

Formulate your goal, what you want to happen in your life. Do you wish to manifest success? How, you may ask yourself, is that success to be manifested? What must happen in the double? What is the bedrock underlying your feet? What do you wish to be made real in the world? What are the dreams or fantasies that power it? Asking these questions allows you to choose your animals with intent, with guided intuition. Turtle may come to you from the south, grounding your manifestation securely. But you read turtle's story again, you think about turtle, turtle appears in a vision or a dream, and greets you for deeper insight. You need to have an idea of what you want and to picture it in your mind's eye. Choose the energy or character from the directions and combine it with the purpose from your animal for your goal to be manifested.

For example, when we made a medicine wheel for the Path of the Feather, we looked at all the stones and chose the human figures to go in the center. That way our families will hear the ancient ones and change their consciousness, to heal themselves, others, and the earth. We placed owl in the east as a prayer for each person who reads the book to see inward. We placed lion in the south to help each reader have passion for their work. We placed bear in the west to help each reader be a healer and let go of what they fear. We placed turtle in the north for grounding.

For more spontaneous manifestation, put each animal down intuitively and then read about them and let them tell you their story. Ask yourself, "Why did I put that animal down?" Don't worry about directions as you put the animal down; place the animal wherever it feels right. When you place the animals, you do not have to know why you chose them. You can place them quickly without rational thought.

— Do a guided imagery. Close your eyes. Imagine yourself in the center of an earth medicine wheel. Call in the animals; invite them into your sacred circle. Speak within yourself clearly. Stand tall in the center of the medicine wheel. Chant and sing your songs. Now think of what you want to manifest. See it, touch it, smell it, hear it. Feel the vision of what you want in your whole body. Open your eyes and look around; see how beautiful the world is. Now take the medicine wheel kit and create a medicine wheel with confidence. Know that each animal brings you its wisdom and holds your wheel. In this will be your magic.

- Take the first stone and place it in the center. This animal holds your vision in the spinning wheel. Say your vision out loud. Now pause, breathe deeply, close your eyes, and visualize this spirit animal standing before you. This is real. The animal sees you. It has come to receive your vision as your offering.
- Take the next stone and place it in the east. This animal takes your vision to the beginning of the spin. Say your vision out loud. Now pause, breathe deeply, close your eyes, and visualize this spirit animal standing before you. This animal will begin the journey. It will receive your vision and call it to life.
- Take the next stone and place it in the south. This animal will take your vision into the light. Say your vision out loud. Now pause, breathe deeply, close your eyes, and visualize this spirit animal standing before you. This animal will journey with you into the brightness of the day so that you will be seen and known in the world as who you are. This animal will be your companion as your vision is manifest.
- Take the next stone and place it in the west. This animal will hold your dreams. It will complete your journey. Say your vision out loud. Now pause, breathe deeply, close your eyes, and visualize this spirit animal standing before you. It will hold your dream. It will allow you to find a place of rest and restoration for your body. It will keep your vision safe within the rhythm of the night and the day. While you sleep, the vision will continue to grow.
- Place the next stone in the north. This animal will take your vision back into the void and out again to manifest it to the world. Say your vision out loud. Now pause, breathe deeply, close

your eyes, and visualize this spirit animal standing before you. In the void, your vision takes on power and becomes part of the collective vision. It becomes larger than you. When your vision comes out, it can spread all over the earth. You can't work all alone; you need the world to make your visions come true.

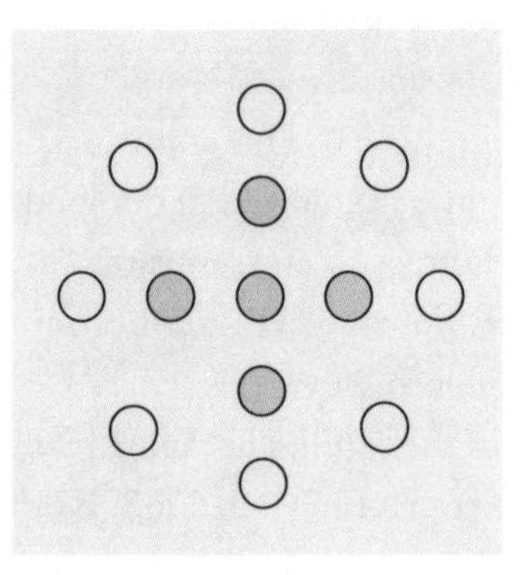

After you have placed the power animals of the first two rings faceup, place the other animals in the outer circle facedown. Begin in the east and move around the medicine wheel clockwise, southeast, south, southwest, west, northwest, north, and northeast. As in all the medicine wheels, the helper animals hold sacred space and are the guardians. By placing the animals facedown without looking at them, the outer circle represents all the animals of the world. They can be any animal, so they invite each animal to be in your medicine wheel (see illustration).

To do this medicine wheel quickly, you can use only five stones. You can start with the stone in the center and do the four around it without setting up the outer circle. You have already set up the outer circle in earlier medicine wheels. You have created the sacred space that surrounds you.

Mary tells us of a vision that came to her. During the day, she made a medicine wheel for manifestation. She placed buffalo in the center for abundance and nurturing. But the wheel was incomplete; there was something that was not happening. That night at two in the morning, she woke with a start. In front of her, in her bedroom, was a great buffalo spirit. Mary says, "He came in thunder, a stampede of thousands, a great buffalo spirit that stood in front of me and looked directly into my eyes. He was seventeen feet tall, huge. He was stern, wild. I looked around me, then, and saw a great buffalo shaman. He did a ritual to the side as I stood before buffalo spirit. There were buffalo people doing chants and dancing on the ridge in a distance. I was dressed as a wolf, with fur and wolf skins all over me. The huge buffalo scared me out of my wits. He said, 'Come with me, I will take you over the edge. Come to the place where the buffalo died. We will sacrifice ourselves for the Path of the Feather. We offer ourselves in sacrifice to you so the path will be worn again. We have sacrificed ourselves in thousands for the people. The buffalo will never return in the physical world in the numbers we were. We will return in spirit if you do exactly what we tell you to do. I will show you how to make your medicine wheel sacred. Come and listen.'

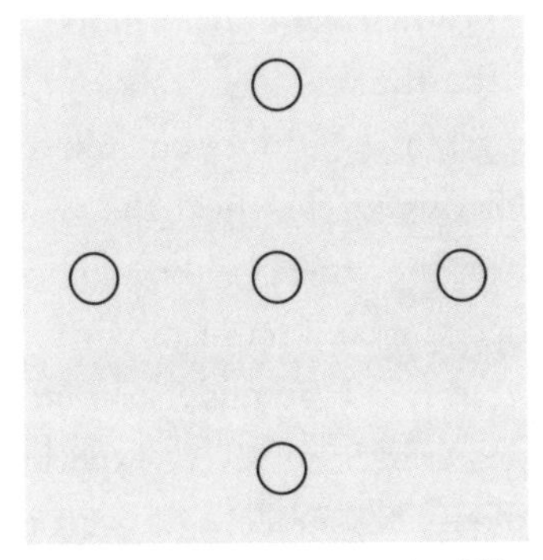

"Then I was in a medicine wheel. Each animal came to me and spoke to me. The animal in the east told me that he would bring the beginning. The animal in the south told me she would bring the wheel into light. The animal in the west told me he would make the wheel while I slept. The animal in the north told me she would take my vision into the void and bring it out again with the power of the consciousness of the collective world."

When the buffalo snorts and you hear the thunder of a stampede, the vision appears. But the buffalo in the vision is not a talking buffalo. It does not talk to you in words like a cartoon figure. You sit up and hear the wisdom of earth speaking to you; you hear the words go through your mind. You understand them; you decipher and translate what you receive into your own language. Your mind can understand it; you know for certain it is true. It is a powerful, real, lived experience. When you are receiving the thoughts, you feel as if you are in an altered state of consciousness, like a trance or a dream.

We had made a medicine wheel for manifestation. It was incomplete, and the spirit animal appeared in the night in a vision to tell us how to finish it. The medicine wheel is just the beginning of the process in which the spirit animal appears and tells you specific things to do. This is the magic of the medicine wheel. When you make a medicine wheel, nothing seems to be happening, but the spirit animals come to you and change your life.

So it is with the other medicine wheels. When you make a medicine wheel for sacred space, your life will become sacred as the wheel is being made and—more important—afterward. When you ask a question of the medicine wheel oracle, you will receive an immediate answer, but answers will come to you from spirit animals for the rest of your life.

The Medicine Wheel Allows the Abundance of the Universe to Flow through You

The medicine wheel creates a tool through which the abundance of the universe flows through you. The medicine wheel is the vehicle to manifest your affirmations and goals. It takes your vision and helps it to become reality in the world.

The medicine wheel is a channel of grace that creates Her reality in the world. We call upon the animals and the ancient ones to help. We call in the powers and energies of the earth to help. The wheel makes you part of something much larger that is growing and expanding. Then abundance of the universe flows through you. Your wishes become reality in harmony with the universe.

Medicine Wheels for Specific Purposes

You can make a medicine wheel for many specific intentions in your life: to see more deeply, to find your purpose, for energy and harmony, for relationships and your family, to help save animals, to have power, to manifest visions, to write books, to help tap into your creativity. You can make a medicine wheel to manifest something specific in your life, to help your career, to make your home, to heal yourself or others, or for protection.

In any of these medicine wheels for a specific purpose, you choose your own animals. Look at the chart and see what each animal stands for. Pick the animal that has the energy you need right now. Then read the story of the animal, and if it is what you need, place it in your wheel.

A Medicine Wheel for Energy and Harmony

In a medicine wheel for energy and harmony, the animals stand for their own energy. Mary says, "As I place each animal in my medicine wheel, I pray for that energy to come to me in my life. For example, for me the lion often stands for manifestation, and when I place it, I think about what I want to manifest. When I place the bear, I think about what needs to be healed. When I place the turtle, I think about how to ground myself in my life. When I place the owl, I think about seeing inward. Each time I do the medicine wheel, my life is different, and it evolves within me."

A Medicine Wheel for Relationships and Family

Mary makes medicine wheels all over her house. She says, "I make one in my bathroom with a serpent in the center to stand for birth and rebirth. I put animals down for each member of my family, a different animal for each. A wolf for my daughter, an eagle for my son, a bear for my baby, a buffalo for my husband, and an owl for myself. This medicine wheel helps create my new home, foster family harmony, and nurture the family members. As I place the animals, I ask them to bring together my family, to manifest harmony and grace."

You can make a medicine wheel for being a mother. To do this, put a mother and baby in the center. You can make a medicine wheel for fertility, for pregnancy, and to make a happy, healthy baby. The medicine wheel calls in the guardians to bring the baby, or protect the baby. In this medicine wheel, Mary uses a symbol of a woman as the figure for Mother in the center, the Woman who gives birth to the earth. In the medicine wheel for mothering, we often use the woman figure or imagine that the specific animal has a baby. We have Zuni fetishes with babies that we use, too. We use the bear for healing, the serpent for fertility. Each of these animals is our own. You may use them or choose your own.

You can build a medicine wheel and put figures in the center that symbolize your friendships. This kind of medicine wheel can be used for any relationship. It can be used to strengthen or heal a marriage. It can bring you a new relationship or mend a hurt. For this purpose, place figures or things about the relationship in the center of the medicine wheel as your offering.

You can make a medicine wheel to bring you a relationship or a lover. The animals will bring you together. They bring the ancient archetypal lovers to earth and teach you the ways coupling happens. If you look at the way the animals mate, they tell you about types of relationships and bring you the relationships you desire.

A nurse of Mary's acquaintance told of how, in the course of her busy day, she goes into each patient's room, gives medicines, and makes entries to the chart. People are soothed by her presence and never want for care. Every night she goes home and makes a medicine wheel. Her spirit animal is the deer, and at night she dreams of a deer running in graceful spirals around an ancient tree. She feels herself spinning spirally, dancing. In the morning she moves softly with her children, seeing them with eyes of gentleness and beauty. When she goes to work, she moves like a deer. She moves between the rooms with grace and fluidity.

A Medicine Wheel for Protection

You can build medicine wheels to create a shield of protection around yourself and your family. Build your medicine wheel and put yourself in the center. Put the animals in the four directions. The animals in this medicine wheel are guardians who protect you from harm, from injury, from illness. People usually choose fierce animals for protection. The lion, bear, and wolf are chosen more often than the horse or buffalo. But this is personal and subtle. A lizard or alligator can protect you from climate variations, an ant from drought. Again, the choice is yours. Make it.

You can build a huge medicine wheel around your house, as the woman in the story below did, using representative stones to protect it from wind, fire, flood, even from earthquakes or hurricanes. The huge medicine wheel protects the house from fierce turbulence and from harm from the elements.

In rural Florida, an elderly woman watched anxiously as floodwaters rose around her house. With the help of her sons, she piled up dirt to make dikes to stop the rising water. Her sons wanted her to leave, but this was the home in which she raised her children. She wasn't leaving. Figuring that she had done all she could in the physical world, she made a medicine wheel. Calling on the spirit world, she asked for the house to be saved if it was in harmony with nature. She went to each of the four directions around her house, where she grounded her wheel with a large, ancient rock. On each rock, she did a ritual.

In the east, she prayed for change. She wrote prayers for protection to keep her house from flood, and buried a bird claw to take her prayer to heaven.

In the south, she put a lion and a cup for fire. Her prayer was, "May there be a gift of fire so that the water comes to quench it."

In the west, she put the bear and a rose quartz stone as big as her heart. The bear was her protector, and she gave him her heart. She asked him to bring the power of the bear to the water.

To the elderly lady, the north was the void. She put gifts of seeds and stones there to broadcast to the void that her wish was in harmony with the earth.

She created a path of feathers to make sacred space. She called in the spirits and the elements to honor them, and then followed the path of the feathers. Without the flood she never would have thought to do any of these things. Her fears of the flood and of the darkness gave her wisdom she'd never had before.

Finally, ritual and action became one for her. She went to water board meetings and found out that the flood was caused partially by a farmer who was pumping out a field. She negotiated with the water board and the farmer to stop the pumping. The waters receded, but she was galvanized. The saving of her house became part of saving the whole wetlands and the watershed. It became part of saving the earth.

Making a Medicine Wheel for Healing Illness

Michael often makes medicine wheels with patients who are interested in shamanism. "I make a medicine wheel around them in my office or in their homes. I choose the animals for them based on what they want or need. Sometimes I take my patients to sacred sites and make medicine wheels with them. I cover them with flower petals, placing them in the center of the medicine wheel. We go to the spring coming out of the mountain near my home or at the mountaintop in the east, the redwoods in the south, the ocean in the west or the Miwok village in the north. I take my patients and we walk into each place, make a small medicine wheel, and do a ceremony. It can take half a day. It is like a healing pilgrimage. We often see animals—owls, deer, even bobcats or mountain lions. It is powerful and healing for me and my patients."

I remember one healing very clearly.

The woman had ovarian cancer. She came to us to learn how to make medicine wheels for healing. She chose the bear for healing, and put him in the center. She chose the owl for seeing inward, and put her in the east for change. She said that cancer had changed her whole life—like a wind, it had blown her to a new place—and now she needed to look within. She chose the serpent, and put her in the south for passion and fire. She wanted healing energy she could find. She chose the deer, and put him in the north for grounding and speed to take her into the void. She needed speed to act fast.

She made the medicine wheel around herself, and lay in the

center with a small serpent on her belly over the scar from her surgery. She closed her eyes. This is what she saw: "I saw myself in the center of a circle of energy, of light. It glowed like a sacred fire. The bear was standing on his hind legs. He said to me, 'I will bring the power of the earth to help you heal. I will bring in the animals to protect you, and I will give you courage and power to be on your healing path.' The owl said to me, 'I will open your eyes to look inward. I will let you see the darkness inside without fear.' The serpent said, 'I will move your healing energy up your spine and throughout your body. I will move the energy to where you need to heal.' The deer said, 'I will carry your prayer into the void and out again to manifest.'" She was no longer alone. She could speak to her helpers as she underwent her ordeal.

A Medicine Wheel for Strength and Courage

Mary tells this story: "When I was doing a television show for my book *Creative Healing,* I was nervous. It was a top-rated show, and I was alone. To help allay my fears, I closed my eyes and asked the bear to come. I did guided imagery to become the bear, and I saw out of her eyes. I became the bear. I felt her fur, her strength, and her courage.

"By the time the show began, I was no longer afraid but instead felt strong and invincible. I had faith in myself and in my ability to do what I needed to do. The show went great! It was my first big talk show and I was with my bear. I felt strong and empowered."

Medicine Wheel Activities

There are many activities that you can do with the medicine wheel to deepen your spiritual practice. Each one uses the medicine wheel to make your life sacred and enhance your path as a shaman.

The Offering

Each time you make a medicine wheel, give an offering of something and put it in the center of the wheel. It may be yourself, the work you do, or something else you value. You are offering the earth and Great Spirit a gift. As you make the offering, purify yourself, honor your ancestors and their pain and suffering. As you make your offering, give thanks and ask for nothing back in return.

You can offer your parenting. If you do not have children, offer something else you have given birth to—something else you have brought forth in effort. Make it something from you, from within your greatest gift, make it rich and abundant. Hold forth what you have done, and say, "I offer this to the medicine wheel." Offering it makes it part of your sacred act. If you are a parent and offer your child, your work as a parent becomes sacred work. If you put a product of your work in the medicine wheel, your work becomes shamanic and sacred.

The Quest to Heal

In this activity, you use the medicine wheel to receive healing energy in your own life, someone else's, or for the living earth. When you create the medicine wheel, write down what you want to be healed, and put it under the center stone. Meditate on your intention for the entire day. Imagine your request is a sacred spiral, a vortex of healing energy that flows through you, into the center of the medicine wheel and through to the earth. From the earth, the energy comes back up as a beautiful spring, a flower that emerges to heal.

Orientation on Your Sacred Path

The medicine wheel can reinforce the lesson that wherever you are, you are on your sacred path. To do this, orient yourself to the directions of the compass, wherever you are. Learn them for your home; learn the directions when you travel, stay in hotels, or visit friends. Pay attention to where the sun is in the sky, where the stars are up above, and when the moon rises and sets. Orient yourself to where you are on the earth at any given time. This exercise is important for a shamanic way of knowing. You must be oriented on the earth to know where you are in visionary space and find out where you are going. The directions in physical space have energies that together create balance in spiritual space.

Seeing out of the Eyes of the Animals

To develop a totally new perspective, try seeing out of the eyes of your favorite power animal. Get to know your animal well. Go to zoos, watch nature programs, find out about its life and habitat. Get to know the animal's way of moving, seeing, its way of breathing. See your world, your neighborhood, your home, as if you were the animal. You'll find the world looks different through new eyes.

Making Your Medicine Wheel Personal

Make your medicine wheel your own story by integrating carved animals or fetishes representing your past vision quests into it. As you begin to make medicine wheels and listen to your spirit animals, visions will come to you. If you see a bear eating salmon, as Michael did in his story at the beginning of the book, you could find a bear fetish eating salmon or something similar. Whatever your story and visions, there is something you can put in the medicine wheel that portrays the experience. If you are making a medicine wheel for your family, incorporate a sculpture of a family. If you are in love, find a sculpture of lovers. If you are making a business, include a symbol for what you are doing. Jewelry often symbolizes important life events and can occupy a powerful place on your wheel. You could put a ring given to you by your partner to honor your bond, or a bracelet given you by your children to symbolize your parenting. When you put things in the medicine wheel that are precious to you, the wheel takes on more meaning and emotion. You transfer to it the importance you place on that object or what it represents. Invite animals to come to your medicine wheel that we do not include in this small book. Make your own stones for them. Find fetishes, feathers, rocks from trips, or drawings of your animals to include in your medicine wheel. Populate your medicine wheel and make it a community. Eventually your medicine wheel becomes a work of art, overflowing with objects of meaning to you. Then it is yours.

Make a Medicine Wheel That You Can Walk Around

Make a big medicine wheel, at least five feet around. Place your animals or other objects in each direction. You could even use rocks to represent the points of the compass. Walk around the medicine wheel and go into a quiet state of mind. Take a deep breath and be silent. Each time you walk around the wheel, feel yourself becoming more connected to the medicine wheel. Touch the stones, and ask for messages to come to you as you walk your path as a shaman. Make this medicine wheel a sacred site, a place where you find a stronger connection to the earth's energies. Sit in the center of your medicine wheel and allow the energy of the earth to flow through you. Ask for messages to come to you to make you a shaman and tell you who you are.

Medicine Wheels in Nature

Find a medicine wheel naturally created by nature. It may be made of rocks, it can be an ancient grove of trees. It can be the circle of a river's bend, a rock outcropping, a natural depression in the earth. As you search for it, ask for a message to come to you from the pilgrimage. Ask what you are to do. Pray and give thanks, listen for thoughts to come to you about the pilgrimage. Look for any animals that appear.

Go to the center of the wheel and ask for the gift of the land and of the spirit animals. Walk to each direction, and make an offering. Then ask for a gift from each direction. As you walk, imagine the animals walking with you. Accept what you find in nature as your gifts—a sight of an animal, sacred animal tracks, or a feather. Speak to the animals you see or hear in your thoughts, and listen to the thoughts that come back to you. That is the spirit animal speaking to you as a shaman.

The Shaman Quest

Go to an ancient sacred site like a ceremonial mound or stone circle. Orient yourself to the four directions. Give thanks to Great Spirit and ask for what you want to come to you. Walk three times around the site. On the first circle ask who you are. On this spiral you see your weakness, fear of this work. You may see pain on the first spiral, and release it. On the second spiral you begin to glimpse who you are without your pain. You start to see what you are to do. On the third spiral, you begin to see clearly, your path is unfolding in front of you, you see what you are to do. Give thanks. On this last spiral, you will feel connected to the earth and hear Her speak to you.

Becoming a Shaman

THE UNDERWORLD

AFTER YOU HAVE become familiar with the medicine wheel we can begin some of the more difficult work of the shaman: going to the underworld.

The underworld is different for each of us since it is representative of our own dark spaces and fear of death. This world is the underbelly of the light world. At times it holds the place of our pain and disappointment, our sadness, loss, and rage. What follows is one woman's very personal experience of the underworld.

"It was pain, a deeply intense and dying pain. I looked inward and saw myself. My figure was broken, distorted, diffuse, crumpled, crying, and bleeding. It was me, but it felt like 'her.' This figure was my despair, uncensored and unintellectualized. The moment I released this image, I stepped back and looked. What I saw was an aspect of myself I couldn't face. It was so ugly. Yet I felt calm and detached. I had let go on an intense emotional and physical level. I saw that the image had captured and contained a moment that now had passed. I had an incredible insight. I had moved past this ugly image. I realized I was witnessing my own transformation.

"In the shamanic process of facing the darkness, I reconstructed my inner self. I manifested movement beyond a place where I had been stuck. As I immersed myself in the process, I not only became who I always wanted to be—a part of myself I had neither acknowledged nor honored—but also allowed myself to glimpse who I really was, and I turned into her. I am strong and powerful, beautiful and whole."

Go into the Underworld with Your Spirit Animal Helpers

The underworld is found in the deepest crevices and darkest shadows of the earth. This place within is so dark that no shaman would go in without the protection of their animal guides. It is the animals, the ancient ones, and the tree spirits who will bring you back. If you are willing to explore the darkness within the corridors in your own mind, you can become a shaman. The wounds of your past, the patterns that are dysfunctional in your life, the legacies of recurring themes from your family—these are the elements of your darkness. Lay down your life and be willing to go into the darkness.

Let go and have faith in the process. Darkness manifests itself in the world as ill events and bad people. In the underworld we come to terms with our self-absorption. Use the spirit animal guides—completely selfless and pure of conscience—as examples to guide you through the primal darkness of your own fears. Allow debts to be repaid, honor the suffering you are given. The earth is trying to wake you up. To understand the suffering of the earth, you must feel your own suffering. We are evolving as more sensitive beings, and now the planet is suffering. The earth has never needed us like this before, and our visions come from the earth to wake us up.

About Protection

Protection is a concern for every shaman. The medicine wheel creates a spiral and offers a veil of protection. The spirit animals are your guardians who protect you as long as the medicine wheel is in place. When you go into visionary space where you are open and vulnerable, you need protection and guardians. The spirit animals hold the space, keep you grounded, and maintain space and time. They will take care of you, love you, and protect you.

Traditional teachers often spoke of spirits that were dangerous and caused illness and misfortune from the underworld. When you make a medicine wheel, you can ask for a barrier of protection around you and your loved ones. You simply ask your spirit animals to protect you and be with you.

Rolling Thunder used to tell Michael, "You cannot be so open; all spirits out there are not friendly. You need protection." Michael asked him what to do. He said, "Ask for the Great Spirit to protect you. Make a bubble of protection around yourself when you work. Keep spirits from other people out of your body by making your boundaries solid."

Death and Rebirth

The Path of the Feather teaches about the inevitable cycle of death and rebirth. All animals die. The ancient ones have died. Our bodies will die, and our loved ones will die. The Path of the Feather calls your ancestors to you and they will sometimes speak of death. They will also help you deal with the death of your loved ones and your animals.

You can see the spirit animals of one who is dying. You can travel into death with them, and help them through the journey. The Path of the Feather also is about the return of the light. When you come back into your body after a vision, or when a birth occurs, you can also assist the spirits as they come across in this direction. You can take them across into the life of the body as yourself or as your spirit animal. The path of the shaman allows you to transcend death, walk across the membrane to the other side, and return with your visions. It is essential to leave what is comfortable and move into the darkness, to merge with your own suffering. Only then will you emerge into the light. The shamanic path is one of healing and renewal. The medicine wheel is your tool, the spirit animals your companions and helpers. The shaman sees across the boundaries of death and rebirth. The shaman is he or she who can see the spirits.

Saving Habitats and Animals

The Path of the Feather's most vital purpose is to save animals and their disappearing habitats. The medicine wheel is our seed of change, one which we hope will initiate change in your life and in the world.

Everywhere on earth, wild animals and wild places are being destroyed. Soon we will only be able to see animals in zoos and preserves unless we can reverse this process of destruction. Ironically, sometimes animals are killed for their powerful healing powers or religious importance. The time for ritualistic killing of wild animals is long past, and we must create new ceremonies that let us speak to the animals without harming them. Each animal is a gift from the spirit. Each time you find a feather, let it remind you that the animals are threatened.

Both Christianity and Judaism teach that we have dominion over the animals. The time is long overdue for a spirituality that protects animals and their habitats. Our wish is that you will learn to see out of the eyes of the spirit animals and fully understand what has been taken from them, what might be gone forever. In turn, we will devote some of the money earned from this book to the preservation of habitats.

The medicine wheel offers a new spirituality and a life path that cherishes the earth. It's almost as if we take the destruction of the earth around us for granted. Perhaps we feel there is little we can do, but the rituals in *The Path of the Feather* can guide you and put you directly in touch with the spirit animals. In the Path of the Feather, dominion over the animals is translated to stewardship and care for the animals.

Beyond your work with the medicine wheel, you might join a preservation organization, or raise money for an endangered species where you live. People like you who watch and protect the animals are their saviors. This is some of the most important work you can do. As you watch the eagle in her nest, ask yourself, Is this eagle endangered, and what can I do to protect her?

The Sacred Earth around Us

While you can make a meaningful medicine wheel anywhere, they are more powerful when centered on a sacred site. The site can be as simple as a special spot in your own backyard. Alternatively, you might make a pilgrimage to an ancient site like Stonehenge. Your world is filled with natural sacred sites such as springs, caves, mountains, and old-growth trees. A sacred place changes our worldview and helps us feel connected to the earth and the spirit world.

Rivers and Springs

If you can't make a special trip to visit a sacred site, perhaps you can find a river or spring near where you live. Rivers and springs are the circulatory system of the earth. Ancient people often lived on or near waterways, where they drew upon the energy of the living water. Water rituals are performed for purification and healing. Springs are magical places and are frequently known to have curative powers.

Ancient Trees

Despite the destructive force of uncontrolled lumbering and clear-cutting of forests, old-growth trees still remain in many parts of the world. Some of the trees that survive today have been living on earth from the time before Christ. These trees are the oldest living beings and they have extraordinary wisdom. They are home to the ancient ones and are deeply sacred.

Once Michael was walking near his house with his teacher, Rolling Thunder, who said, "Listen to one sentence perfectly." He pointed to a tree, and said, "This is the grandfather plant; it is in charge of all the others. Don't hurt that plant or all the others will die." Michael listened to the last sentence perfectly and he has never forgotten Rolling Thunder's message: Never hurt the grandfather tree or the forest is at risk.

Even in your own backyard, you can find the grandfather/grandmother tree. He is the oldest tree in the neighborhood, responsible for all the others. Visit this tree during your own ceremony and leave a special offering out of respect and thanks. This now marks your own sacred site.

Healing Rituals on Sacred Sites

The Ancient Sacred Sites

Whenever you do a ritual, you are participating in the most ancient form of worship. For millions of years, humans and their ancestors have made medicine wheels and spoken to spirit animals. When you go on the Path of the Feather, you enter the realm of all those who have gone before you. There are resonances—patterns of energy—that remain long after a ritual act has been performed. We believe that wherever ritual has been done, its prayers and thought forms remain forever. When you do a similar ritual you reconnect to those resonances and you experience what has come before. When you do a medicine wheel, you are part of all the medicine wheels that have ever been done; when you speak to an owl, you join all the owl energy of the past.

Resonance is especially important for people who live in large cities where it is more difficult to find ancient trees and animals. Before the city was built it was a forest, a riverbank, a mountain. Before the city was built, there were bears, lions, and eagles. The spirits of the ancient animals and shamans still surround you as resonances. The animals may be gone now, but their spirits await your ritual and they will return.

Resonance is even more obvious when you do ritual on an ancient sacred site like Stonehenge, Avebury, or Chaco Canyon. The energy of these sites enters us, making our healing more effective. The ancient spirits who did the rituals to heal in the past return and speak to us, lending us their power.

Making a Big Medicine Wheel as a Vision Quest

A man tells us this story: "I went to the shell mound in Cedar Key, Florida, to make my large medicine wheel. The mound was built by ancient ones thousands of years ago. In my imagination I saw their rituals and felt the history of this place. I walked around the mound the first time. It was about a mile. I knew the ritual would take a while. I asked for a gift during each spiral. In the first spiral, all I thought about were my worries and insecurities. I felt silly. I wondered if this exercise was doing anything. During the second spiral I felt better. I thought about my work, about what I did best. I saw its beauty. During the third spiral I heard a voice.

She told me my work was precious. She told me which aspects of it were most beautiful, and showed me how they would heal myself and the earth. During the last spiral I was deep in a trance. I was tired, too. She blessed me and told me to continue my work in a sacred way. She told me who I was and what I was to do. When I thought about it later, I realized that the process went from being in pain to seeing who I was to honoring my work as sacred to being blessed and loved. This sacred medicine wheel walk changed my life."

Making a very large medicine wheel calls forth Her voice and the voices of the ancient ones. Making a large medicine wheel on the earth transforms your landscape from an ordinary material world to one that is mystical, sacred, and visionary. This is a medicine wheel to make your landscape sacred.

To make this medicine wheel, you need time, space, and intention. If there are places in your landscape that you are attracted to, that you look at on the horizon with a desire to know what is there, go there. You are discovering a place; use maps, find out what is in that direction. It can be an ancient ceremonial mound, a river, a mountain. You can't see it but it's there. It can take a day's journey or several days. Use your intuition to decide which direction to go and what to do there.

The center of your first large medicine wheel will be the place you are most often—your office or your home. You have already created a physical resonance in this place, it is the center of your vortex. The goal is to make the vortex very large, miles wide, the entire vista of the landscape you are residing in.

Begin from your center. Go east. When you go to the place where the earth's energy is most powerful, place a feather making the ground sacred. Build a small medicine wheel on each site out of stone and leave it there. Build another with your kit or fetishes, and take it with you. Leave an offering, a feather or special stone, jewelry, or an object that is precious in your life. You can leave a carved fetish animal that you have used and has meaning. Be there, stay there. Now journey to the south. You can travel days or hours. The medicine wheel can be two miles or several hundred miles wide. In each place do the ritual.

MARY:

"I was making a huge medicine wheel that was as big as the state of New Mexico. First I started in Sante Fe in the east and made a medicine wheel at my friend's house. Next, I went to Acoma Pueblo in the south where I met a woman who made pots with bears on them and bought several from her. Then I went to Zuni Pueblo in the far south and I picked out a double-eagle fetish for seeing clearly in writing this book. Next, I went to Canyon de Chelly in the west. I went into the canyon with a Navaho guide whose grandfather was a medicine man. I held my baby up to the rising sun and then took my baby into the canyon. We saw double eagles flying. We saw petroglyphs and together we put our hands on the cliff wall.

"Then we drove across the painted desert heading far north, to Aztec Ruin, a national park. After our long journey I was very disappointed to find the ruin closed for the day, but I was determined. My visions had led me here and this was an important part of my medicine wheel.

"I woke early the next morning and returned to Aztec Ruin again at dawn. The ruin was still closed. I was driven to visit this kiva. Despite my fear and the closed gates, I went down into the large kiva. I stood boldly in the center of the structure, watching. The light shifted and the silence was full. It was that magical time in between the night and day. Then, in the shadows, I saw the ancient ones emerge. A circle of elders gathered around me. I saw an old grandmother, eyes sparkling. The rest of them were solemn and still, and there was a heaviness and density in the room. The grandmother looked at me and, while her mouth did not move, I could hear her voice. She seemed so familiar, as if she knew me. I felt she knew me on a level I did not even know myself. She spoke to me with great force: 'You are one of the ancient mothers of the earth.' Silence followed and I could feel all the eyes upon me.

"Suddenly, I knew who I was. My body vibrated with energy. I heard it again. 'You are one of the ancient mothers of the earth.' I looked down at my hands and lifted them up into the air. I said to myself, 'I am one of the ancient mothers of the earth.' Now I was not afraid. My life had forever changed. I heard for the first time the fullness of my own voice. The elders gave me the gift of my own voice and in its wisdom I knew who I was in the world. I am an ancient mother. Next time, when I lifted my baby up, I realized it was true, I was really one of the ancient mothers of the earth, and all the mothers of the earth were with me, saying, 'You are one of us.' My medicine wheel had become a ceremony with the ancient ones. It was unexpected, unplanned. It simply was.

"In the center of my medicine wheel was Chaco Canyon. There I gave myself and my baby as an offering. I put him in a bearskin and held him up to the sun, in the big kiva at Chaco. I showed him how to make his first big medicine wheel. It told him he will have visions of ancient ones and the earth, and I said, 'May you have energy of bear, may I be a mother who makes the world better just by having you.'

"For me, this big medicine wheel was a quest for my own visions. I walked through a closed door and came away forever changed. The vision came from making the huge medicine wheel in each direction. It resonated with the body of the earth, with the ancient ones and spirit animals. They spoke to me in the pure voice of the living earth."

The Four Spirals of Becoming a Shaman

You become a shaman by living your life as a vision quest. In this process you will spiral four times. With each spiral, you go around the medicine wheel of your life, deeper and deeper in your shamanic life.

The First Spiral: Your Medicine Wheel at Home

In the first spiral, you start by making your personal medicine wheel. During this practice, your life becomes enchanted. Suddenly, the animals come back to life. Look for animals wherever you go. Look in the forests, on the side of the road, on your way to work. Even in the city, there are animals all around you. Look for the hawk high overhead. When you see her, you will know she has come to you. Enchantment is possible for everyone. It is a celebration of your body and your senses. It is the liberation of your spirit. Pray for the animals to come, call for them. When you see the owl, you know you are on the right path.

The Second Spiral: A Medicine Wheel in Nature

Begin this spiral by building your medicine wheel in nature. Find a place in your own life that is sacred to you. It can be a grove of old trees, a river, a mountain, a cave, a stone circle. Then build a circle with stones or build one in your mind. Create a sacred medicine wheel on the earth itself, making it larger than the one at home. Call the animals in the four directions. Look around you and see who lives there. Then ask to see out of the eyes of the animals, and you will see their world. The animals know when you do this work with love, and they will come to you and tell you their stories.

Allow yourself to be taken in by the second spiral, surrender to it. You slip through the membrane. You leave your home and go into the forest. You walk slowly and give yourself time to listen and see.

The Third Spiral: Make a Huge Medicine Wheel

Within the next spiral, you will make a living medicine wheel by visiting a sacred site in each of the four directions. Each site is one part of the medicine wheel, just like one stone in your wheel at home. When you have selected four sites, make a medicine wheel in each direction. Find the sources of energy in the landscape around you, and ask for the earth's energies to empower you. You go into Her body and you hear Her song in nature.

Go to an old tree, go next to a bubbling brook, go to a beach, and go to a meadow. Take the medicine wheel stones from your home and create your medicine wheel in nature. To do this, you have to travel, but everything within the large circle of your medicine wheel becomes sacred. Your life and world, in turn, become sacred.

The Fourth Spiral: Your Small Medicine Wheel as an Offering

In the last spiral, go back to the little medicine wheel at home and build it again. Say a prayer and give thanks. Pray for its blessings to bring forth your own visions. Make an offering to your medicine wheel, placing something you value in the center. When She returns it to you, it will be enchanted. Everything you receive is a gift from the spirit world. Everything you do is an offering. Your work is a gift; what you do is an offering.

Your Shamanic Initiation

The vision quest is the basic tool to invite shamanic visions. You've gone on many already. By now you've realized that on the Path of the Feather, your whole life is a quest for visions. This imagery exercise will take you on a specific vision quest into Her heart, preparing you for your initiation as a shaman.

Close your eyes, take several deep breaths, let your abdomen rise and fall. Enter your imagery space as you have many times before. Now put yourself on a path. Feel your feet touch the earth, smell the fresh air, feel the warm breeze on your face. Walk down the path. It goes downhill slightly. The ground is hard and has small stones in the soil. It is solid and secure. Feel the ground and the grass that is on each side of the path. Walk down the path. It crosses a wooden bridge across a rushing stream. The bridge has stout railings. You can hear your feet echo on the bridge like a drum-

beat as you walk across. If you need to drop something in the water that you want to get rid of you can do that now. You've been on this path before.

The path now goes upward slightly and comes over a rise. Below you is a large meadow. In the center of the meadow is a grassy circle. You've met animals here before. Sit in the circle and wait.

Now imagine that you are thirteen years old. Feel your body, feel your strength, feel your youth. You are on the verge of becoming an adult. Among your group of people, this age marks a rite of passage. It is a special day for you. You have been brought here by the elders to do a vision quest that will inform your life. You know what this is like from talking to older children. You have heard that they all go into the wilderness and find a spirit animal. They find their animal helpers and ancient spirits. The helpers and spirits speak to them and tell them who they are and what they are to do.

The elders speak to you. They say, "You are going on a three-day vision quest. You take only what you can carry. Find a sacred place and sit and wait. Wait for the animals to come to you. Wait and listen. Don't eat if you can help it, don't sleep if you can help it. When the visions come, welcome them and listen and then you will become an adult. All adults of our people have animals as guides."

Now imagine that you walk deep into the forest. As you travel, you find a cave, a high rock, or a mountaintop. You know you are on a journey to find your own visions. You go deeper into the forest, higher up, deeper into the wild places. You have never been so far from home, alone. You find your special place and you sit and wait and wait and wait.

After a long time, an animal comes to you. It comes up to you and looks in your eyes. There are no people here, only you and the animal. It drinks and you drink alongside it. It looks at you and enters your spirit.

Then you start to follow it. It moves silently among the shadows, hunting. You notice how it moves, how it crouches, and pounces. You think, Maybe I am the hunter, maybe I can camouflage myself too. *The animal teaches you to hunt and then it vanishes in a flash. You wonder,* Was it a spirit animal? *You are filled with awe.*

After a long time you see another animal. You see out of its eyes more easily now than with the first. What comes to you if you are alone in the forest, on the mountain, on a river? The animals come and they become your teachers. They teach you about the earth, about life. When you are asleep, the animals call to you, as if offering a challenge. The animals become your guide and the teachers of the sacred wisdom of the earth. This is your vision quest.

Now return to your circle. Join your people. Come back to where you started. Bring your animals with you. Move your feet. You are home. But now, you are an adult. Now you have animal guides to inform your life and tell you who you are and what you are to do.

A Guided Imagery for Your Shamanic Initiation

The shamanic life has been viewed as a calling and a choice. The shaman was called by a vision, which showed the life path ahead. Sometimes they could not stop it from happening to them. Where did the vision come from? In the Path of the Feather, your vision comes from Her, from the earth.

All shamans were initiated into their practice. The initiation was sometimes performed by another shaman and sometimes done in a vision. We have done this exercise with thousands of people in workshops all over the world. In this guided imagery, you can go as far as you want to. In this imagery, you picture your body being taken apart. Some people are not comfortable with this, but it is safe. However, if your intuition tells you to stop, please do so and perhaps try again later. If you feel safe and comfortable you can do the whole exercise. If you want to stop anywhere along the line, stop and rest there.

Make yourself comfortable. Close your eyes, relax, take several slow deep breaths. Let your breathing become slow and even. Feel your abdomen rise and fall as you breathe. Go into your imagery space as you have many times before. Now imagine that you are on a path. It is a path in the forest, a path that is mysterious and beautiful. Feel your feet touch the earth, smell the fresh air, feel the warm breeze on your face.

Walk down the path. It goes downhill slightly. The ground is hard and has small stones in the soil. It is solid and secure. Feel the ground and the grass that is on each side of the path. Now the path crosses a wooden bridge across a rushing stream. The bridge has stout railings. You can hear your feet echo on the bridge like a drumbeat as you walk across. If you need to drop something in the water that you want to get rid of you can do that now.

The path now goes upward slightly and comes over a rise. Below you is a large meadow. In the center of the meadow is a grassy circle. Sit in the circle and wait. With you in the circle are your friends and teachers, people who support you in this work. You have come here today for a special ceremony. It is the day of your shamanic initiation. It is a day full of importance, a day you will long remember. You have been told about this day for many years, and you know what will happen. It is safe and you will only be asked to do what you can.

Now you feel hands behind you lifting you up from the sitting position in the circle. It is the elders, your teachers tapping you to begin. You stand, and they take you into the forest and guide you to a stone. It is the ceremonial stone for shaman initiation used by many who have gone before you. You lie on the stone and close your eyes.

Your elder sings to you. You hear the melody rise and fall. Let yourself drift now, upward, upward. You are swirling now, spinning. Now you are with the owls, the eagles, the hawks. Feel their wings around you. Let them pick you up and take you high in the sky. Feel yourself carried in their talons upward and upward. Now you are taken to a high rock on the top of the highest mountain.

Now the eagle will touch you. The owl will take you apart. Let this go as far as you feel comfortable. Each person has their own natural place to stop. It is safe, but it is up to you. Let the hawk take you apart, let the eagle take your skin off, and your bones apart. Let the owl eat you and reduce you until you are your essence. That may be a jewel, a blue light, dots, energy, a crystal. Then if you wish, let that essence dissolve into endless space and let yourself move outward to the edge of space to fly with creation.

When you are at the end of your travels, come back. You can see a little now as you let yourself come back toward the light, toward the rock. Feel your body pull back together. Let the eagle's wings bring your body together as one now. Let your bones come together, your muscles come back, your skin smooth out. Now your body is back together but it is new and it is completely different. Having seen the essence within, the jewel is still visible, and you are remade as a shaman.

Now the owl takes you in its talons and carries you over the treetops to the tallest tree. There she puts you in her nest with her baby owls. The eagle feeds you and you grow and grow. The hawk feeds you magic jewels and you get brighter and brighter. You stay in the nest in the top of the tallest tree as long as you like, perhaps years.

Now the owl brings you down and puts you back in the circle with your friends. You open your eyes, and see them all around you. Now you can stand and walk back on the path to where you started. You can open your eyes and feel your feet on the ground and you are home. But you are now different. You have been initiated. Your body is magical and healthy. You are on the Path of the Feather.

In the Path of the Feather, your first medicine wheel is the beginning of your initiation. Each time you make a medicine wheel you go deeper into your shamanic initiation. This guided imagery is a vision that helps you go beyond the medicine wheel. Your real initiation is making the medicine wheels and seeing out of the eyes of the ancient ones and the spirit animals. As you become the animal shaman, its powers come to you and you are changed. You have the courage of the bear, the insight of the owl, the grounding of the turtle, the passion of the lion. You are within Her earth and you have access to the power of your own life.

Bringing In the Light

After your shamanic initiation, after you've traveled some distance along the path, after you've met your power animals and heard the voice of the living earth, after you've gone to the underworld and seen that which you fear, you are ready for one of the most powerful of a shaman's activities: bringing in the light, a ritual with deep roots in ancient shamanism. Do not do this activity lightly, for as you travel the Path of the Feather, you will learn that those you meet will ask things of you, just as you ask things of them. Bringing in the light announces that a true shaman is in their midst, and they will expect healing—of the earth, of your community, of yourself—from you. Bringing in the light, like the ordination of a minister, puts the responsibility for your community squarely on your shoulders.

Bringing in the light is a practice that harnesses the sacred energy from your ritual site; it brings incredible energy to you and your medicine wheel. Bringing in the light makes you the center of the medicine wheel, surrounding you with a dome of light that comes up from the earth and down from the sky at once. This ceremony allows you to see Her face. When you make a dome of light, She appears in the center and blesses your work. Bringing in the light heals you and your surroundings.

When you put yourself in the center of the medicine wheel, you are embraced by the earth's love. You are kissed by the ground and caressed by the wind. She who gardens us from above loves you.

Bringing in the light is done with conscious intent. Go to the center of the medicine wheel, close your eyes, and perform the following exercise to bring in the light. When you are illuminated you can hear the animals clearly and your intuition is sharp.

A Guided Imagery Exercise to Bring In the Light

Find a place in nature that is sacred for you. It can be a beach, a clearing in the woods, a hilltop, a mound, or a stone. You can do this exercise alone or with another person. If you bring in the light with a partner, stand apart, look at each other, and do it together.

Stand in the sacred place and pause. Give thanks to Great Spirit for the place. Now close your eyes. Put your arms at your side and relax. Open your eyes. Now slowly, very slowly, raise your arms upward until they almost touch over your head. Now touch your hands together at the top. It is as if you are pointing upward to Her heart. As you raise your arms, see the light from the earth getting brighter and brighter. It is as if you are creating a sacred dome of light around you. The dome of light rises and rises, and when your arms are together at the top, it is complete. Now slowly bring your hands apart and down to each side. This brings the light down over you and the earth and holds it there.

Now stand in the light and feel its beauty and brightness. This is Her light on earth. You can bring in the light whenever you are doing ritual, healing, or making love. Sometimes you can see Her face in the center of the light. It is She who gardens us from above; She who loves us and cares for us always.

You Have a Right to This Teaching

The Knowledge of the Medicine Wheel Comes from the Earth

The knowledge of the medicine wheel comes to you from your own experience. When making the medicine wheel, you will learn things through your thoughts, visions, dreams, and body. Pay attention, and honor what you learn.

You have a right to the teaching of the medicine wheel. What you learn through your own experience is yours. It belongs to no one people because it comes from within you, and from the earth itself. You create your sacred space, and the medicine wheel is the doorway of exploration.

These stories began over five thousand years ago, before the written word, before we became separate peoples. These stories belong to everyone, they have no specific antecedent. Instead, they go back to the very beginning, when we were simple creatures on the earth. There was a time when human consciousness was united, when we looked and saw ourselves, not enemies. The medicine wheel helps us return.

The term *shaman* came from Siberia thousands of years ago. The medicine wheel existed in many cultures thousands of years before people crossed the land bridge from Siberia to settle in North America. None of the material in this book is presented without permission. Shamans from all over the world who shared information with us did so specifically so that we could share it with you. They believe the time has come for these teachings to be available to everyone.

We know that some people do not want the terms *shaman* and *medicine wheel* used by people who are not of first-nations heritage. They have told us that they feel strongly it is being stolen from them like the land. We are sorry that they associate our saying that the earth is sacred with the way some of our ancestors treated them.

We apologize for the way some of our ancestors treated indigenous peoples. We apologize to each person of first-nations descent for the genocide of their people. We believe the sacred earth belongs to everyone and now needs all people working together to heal Her. All people need to save the animals now. All people need a sacred vision.

Do Right Action

This book is about honoring the earth's energy within us, returning people to the wind, the fires, the earth, all the animals—the lion, the bear, the owl, the turtle. We want to bring it all back full circle. Plant the feather in the soil of your own medicine wheel; commit your life as an offering to the earth.

Anything you do is about taking action. It is not just about meditation and making medicine wheels and dreaming; it is about manifesting the vision of the medicine wheel. You need to do something, to take action, to become an activist for what you want to manifest in the world.

You manifest your shamanic goal, you make ceremony in order to make action. The medicine wheels are layers of learning, layers of teaching. They build on each other, then finally you build a huge one in your yard, in your landscape. The medicine wheel goes from being a table in the corner of your living room to becoming your whole life.

A Guided Imagery for the Shamanic Path of Right Action

Close your eyes, take a couple of deep breaths, let your abdomen rise and fall. Go into your imagery space as you have many times before. Now imagine you are looking for an ancient medicine wheel, you have been searching for it all day. You have asked many people where it is, and have walked many paths without finding it. Finally you feel it even before you see it. In front of you is a plateau that is the highest point of land for many miles around you. It is a sacred hilltop with the prairie extending in all directions as far as you can see. Beyond the hilltop are canyons, rivers, a beautiful vista. You realize that you are on the highest hill, that when you look all around, you see the entire landscape. In the center of the hilltop is a medicine wheel of stones. The circle is about one hundred feet across; it is made of stones that feel warm to the touch, that seem to vibrate with power.

Now imagine yourself in the center of the medicine wheel. In your mind's eye, you feel a sacred axis running through you, connected to the earth, all the way to the earth's center. You stand on the top of the plateau, in the center of the medicine wheel; suddenly you feel the earth rotating around you, spiraling through space.

Now bring the earth's energies into your body, into your consciousness, into your life. You look around and the first thing you see is an ancient one on horseback. The figure looks directly into your eyes and recognizes you and knows you. He has come to you to bring you strength and the earth's wisdom. Then you look into the directions. You can feel and see the spirit animals in the landscape of the earth, the lions, tigers, elephants. Wolves, bears, eagles. Owls. You can feel all the animals are living deeply connected to the earth and their consciousness is one with the earth. Their mind has expanded and is very large. It envelops all the places where the humans and animals live. You feel large, as expansive as the wind, the lakes, the rivers. Your body is the earth, trees, rocks; you have become the body of the living earth. You have become Her.

When you stand in the center of the wheel, you feel your feet on the ground. Feel the energy rise up through your legs, feel your body from your legs, your feet up into your pelvis; feel the flame within you getting brighter, through your neck, up through your head, your face, up through you, up the axis into the sky. Imagine yourself glowing with a light that is bright, feel the grace and the love from the earth flowing through your body. Slowly lift your arms up, bringing energy around you, moving energy through space, bringing the light up, feeling it embrace you and envelop you. Feel the flame inside your own heart brighten. The earth is nourishing you, loving you; the energy of the earth is the earth's love. Feel the love flow through you. In your mind's eye, open your eyes and see the landscape transformed into a place in which all things live in balance and harmony, where we live within ourselves with the animals and outside ourselves with the animals. Inside of us, the animals roam. Outside in the landscape, the animals roam. We honor the storms, the sunrise, the tranquil days. All this belongs to us as we belong to it.

The earth is here for you, it is being given to you now. You are receiving the gift of life in the recognition of your life as sacred; it is a gift of the earth. Ask yourself and your spirit animal, "What is the right action?" It is your vision quest. As a shaman, you step forth from this center. Everything you do, see, and touch brings this vision to life.

The ancestor says to you, "We can reclaim the earth's energy and harness the power of the living earth to create a future. Create a future, for the future of your children's grandchildren. We leave a legacy of peace and harmony with the earth, you must leave the same to your children and children's grandchildren."

Medicine Wheel Four: A Medicine Wheel for Right Action

This last medicine wheel of the Path of the Feather is for right action. This medicine wheel is about your commitment to follow the way of the shaman. Without commitment, there can be no right action.

You will make a medicine wheel and plant your feather in the earth as an offering. You can make this medicine wheel outside your home in your yard. If you live in an apartment, you can make the medicine wheel in a space outside or in your apartment, on the edges of a room, or on the decks around it.

Find a sacred place in your personal landscape that is five feet in diameter. Collect stones that are six to eight inches across. Make a medicine wheel with your stones. You can pick stones from all over.

Finally place a feather in the center as the center stone as your offering for your intention of right action.

Use this medicine wheel for ceremony and ritual. Go outside to the east, go outside in the hours as the sun rises. Stand with your feet centered under your body as the sun rises. Raise your hands with the morning sun. Feel yourself reborn on this new day; feel the first rays of the sun caress your face; smell the newness of the day, the dew of the trees; feel the stirring all around you. There are deer and foxes running in the forest, hawks flying in the daylight, the owl sleeping on the branch, resting after a night's hunt. Watch, listen, and sniff the air; this is your new day. Go to the south, the west, the north. Give a prayer as an offering to each direction, see who you are and what you are to do. Do your ritual in the four directions, do ritual as you walk the Path of the Feather.

Stand in the center of your medicine wheel and close your eyes. Look within and ask for the spirit animal to give you a gift of one action. Ask for something that you can do to achieve your goal, to manifest the reality that you want to happen on earth. Then open your eyes and leave the medicine wheel and do it. Start on the first step to create the reality that you have prayed for, been given by the spirit animal, manifested, and now work toward. Go in peace.

This medicine wheel is a sacred circle in which the offering is your life. Your life as an offering is to follow the path of a shaman. Your actions will be the actions of a shaman bringing spirit into physical reality. No matter what you do in life, you are bringing spirit into its form through right action. With your life as your offering, you are truly the shaman walking the Path of the Feather.

As a shaman, the next step is to do right action for humanity and for the community. You now can see into a visionary world and live within the medicine wheel. You are now a wisdom keeper of the medicine wheel. Each one of us has our own piece of the wisdom that makes the world whole, each one of us blends together. Each shaman's vision brings a greater shamanic vision to light. Each person who brings their vision forth, wholeheartedly, with spirit, light, and love is living as a shaman.

The Ichetucknee is a sacred river in northern Florida. It flows from a headspring that is blue and cold, from the heart of the largest freshwater aquifier on earth. It flows pure and crystal clear—a living symbol of cleansing, purification, and holiness. It is a healing spring and has been so for thousands of years. But a tire-burning cement plant is scheduled to be built four miles from the river.

This fact angered a woman. She started kayaking on the river and listening each day to Her songs. She paddled up into each spring and listened to what She had to say. She listened to the voices of the owl, the beaver, the otter, the hawk. She saw the visions of She Who Gardens Us from Above and the old woman who dwelled at the river's headwaters in ancient times.

Then she acted. She built a Web site to help save the river. She sent daily e-mails about environmental health to the governor of Florida. She communicated with people all over the earth who were fighting similar battles. For her, shamanic ritual and activism became one. The rituals of artistry, performance, giving concerts, and writing to the secretary of the Department of Environmental Protection became one. She became a contemporary shaman to stop the cement plant. Her tools were listening to the spirit animals and the springs, making medicine wheels, using the Web and e-mail, going to meetings at the capital, and making his life an embodied prayer.

Doing right action is following the shamanic path, and the shamanic way is right action. Take a feather in your hand, and walk from the center of the medicine wheel. There will be a gentleness in every moment in your life. Hold the feather up, it creates the balance, sensitivity, fragileness. As you hold the feather in all you do, you follow the spiritual shamanic way.

The Feather Is a Symbol of Spirit and Being on the Right Path

You have come to the place in the center of the medicine wheel—the Path of the Feather as a way of being. Your feather is a symbol of your spiritual and shamanic journey. Being on the right path means that whatever you are doing is right action. It is about trusting that what you are doing is right for you and for the earth. The feather is a symbol that the earth honors you, recognizes you, and gives you a gift from its body for what you do. The gift of the feather is the earth's way, in its most gentle form, of honoring you.

In 1999 a group of first-nations people marched five hundred miles in the dead of winter from South Dakota to Yellowstone National Park in Wyoming to save the last herd of free-roaming buffalo. They walked each day in the cold, in the snow. Their elders walked with them; children wrapped in blankets echoed the past marches across the plains for centuries.

At Yellowstone they made a circle and performed a sun dance buffalo ritual that had never been seen by nonindigenous people and had not been done for one hundred years. A man dragged a buffalo skull around the circle. His commitment and the commitment of his people to what they believe was awesome. The pilgrimage and ordeal they underwent to manifest was extreme.

Right action comes from commitment. Your life is a symbolic act no matter what you do. You do everything in spirit space. You can't take anything with you when you die. We have nothing except the faith in ourselves and the commitment to manifest our own life. To do right action, let something flow through you from Great Spirit with commitment. Make a difference by doing something that is not solely for you. Do something that is bigger than you. Do it generously.

Ritual and Right Action Are One

The contemporary shaman does ritual and right action at the same time. He or she is inside the opening where a moment is born, within Her heart. And the shaman enters that moment and helps create it on earth. The shaman acts within the dream that gives birth to the moment. Then they open their eyes and see it on earth. This is shamanic visioning. This is seeing Her vision on earth. They then must do action to manifest it.

The first action is making sacred space.
The second action is finding out what you are to do on the vision quest.
The third action is manifestation through prayer and visioning.
The fourth action is doing right action.

In the prayer to create sacred space, we thank Great Spirit for the earth and for its beauty, and we pray for our goal to be achieved if it is in harmony with Great Spirit's vision.

In the vision quest we call the spirit animals of the four directions and make the sacred medicine wheel. We ask our questions concerning what we are and what our work is to be.

Then we become the spirit animals, see out of their eyes, and ask for their gifts to come to us so we can see deeper and act to heal Her body. We give our offerings and receive Her gifts and we ask for Her will to be manifested on earth.

Finally, in right action we do one sacred act to achieve our goal. We do a piece of art, a group ritual, write a letter, lead a fund-raising event, make posters, make phone calls, get together as one. We make Web sites and set up networks of sacred spiritual energy.

Ritual and right action are one. The shaman is the sacred artist who dreams reality, sees Her face, makes it happen on earth, and connects the people and helps them see the vision too. Ritual and right action are one in Her heart, they are one in our breath, they are one on earth. And then the action and the vision are one in each moment, in each breath.

By making a medicine wheel, you create sacred space, call in the spirit animals and live your life as a shaman on the Path of the Feather. Your life becomes an offering, and the feather is a symbol of that offering.

The medicine wheel is a circle, it is the path that goes around and around in a cycle like going from birth to death. Water comes down as rain, evaporates, and goes back up into the clouds and comes down as rain again. It is the path that goes in a circle like the moon around the earth, the earth around the sun, the galaxies around each other. Eagle sings, "There are sacred circles of feathers. They are our nests for initiation." Your sacred circle of feathers for initiation is the medicine wheel.

Eagle sings: "Return the animals to our role as teachers. We are your guides. The shamans needed us to guide them. We know how to move in the mystery world, the shaman does not. People no longer listen to us. We love to speak. Your ritual is our voice. Doing it will teach you to listen to us again."

The tree with the eagle's nest speaks: "Humans are custodians of the land now. You are all on the land to save it, to take care of it. Do right action, save the habitat and the animals and trees that live here. You are the only ones who can do it."

A man was about to build his house on a beautiful piece of land—the sort of place he had dreamed about his whole life. On the day before construction was to begin, he noticed an eagle's nest in a tree right where his porch would stand. It annoyed him that it was there, and he resolved to cut the tree down. The eagle would just have to move. He walked to the tree and looked up to the top. An eagle feather floated down to him. Now unsure, he made a medicine wheel under the tree to ask the oracle what to do. He prayed for guidance, for knowledge. He closed his eyes and heard in his mind, "Take this feather as a gift. I am Eagle Spirit. I live on your land, and I can protect you and your home. Do not destroy the trees that are my habitat. I will live with you if you leave the trees. I will give you power and vision if you speak to me. We can live in peace as partners." The man moved his proposed house away from the eagle's nest. He left the grove of trees intact, and the medicine wheel under the tallest one. Now he can see the nest from his new home. He can see the eagle take off and soar. With a telescope, he can see her feed her young. In his visions, he can soar, too. His home is more wonderful than he ever had imagined.

You have become connected to the consciousness of the earth. When you see the earth as sacred, you do everything differently. Work to keep the earth there for you, your children, and your children's grandchildren. We connect to the earth by making the medicine wheels, by embodied ceremony. We remember that every choice we make is the seed of the right action because it comes from the center of the medicine wheel. Everything will be protected when you come from that place.

The shaman is he or she who flies into the darkness in the cloud in front of the sun and then emerges into the light. The shaman is one who sees beauty, from flying into darkness without fear. The spirit animals are your teachers. The shaman is you. The Path of the Feather is your road.

Thank you for being with us on the Path of the Feather. We thank you for listening. We honor you for who you are and for all your effort in doing this sacred work. Owl thanks you, bear thanks you, lion thanks you, turtle thanks you. All the animals of the earth thank you for listening to them again and letting them be your teachers. They all call to you and surround you with their love. Relax, take a deep breath, listen to your spirit animals sing to you. Make a medicine wheel in your day. Go in peace.

The Ancient Ones and the Spirit Animals Speak to You

The Animals Speak to You

In *The Path of the Feather*, we share our stories of the animals to get you started on your own path. We do not present our stories as definitive but rather as guidelines for your first medicine wheels. The medicine wheel will guide you to a place where you hear the stories from the animals themselves. In time, the animals will tell you their own stories. The stories we have shared were all told to us by the medicine wheel and by the animals. They are from our experience, not from the tradition of one people or from research.

We have chosen a small number of animals to correspond with the stones, but these are not the only animals. They are the ones that have come to us. When you travel the Path of the Feather, you will find animals that we do not mention. There are many animals to find and to be found by, to listen to and to heed. The puma may come to you. The gopher. The dove. Even the lowly field mouse. They all are messengers, and their words must be honored. The animal that finds you or the animal that you find may be far different from what you expect. You may search for something majestic—a buffalo, a lion—only to receive an animal that surprises you.

Everyone has their own spirit animals. The animals in this book chose us by coming to us in our visions. For Mary, these are the visions she has seen since the owl took her, and the teachings are from the ancient ones. Michael shares the visions he had since his bear took him to the mountaintop. The ancient ones came to him and told him these stories. She had the owl. He had the bear. They collaborated, but the stories originated from the animals.

We make medicine wheels wherever we go. We started with the owl, the lion, the bear, and the turtle. Then we each went into new landscapes and found other animals. The spider came, the otter came, the eagle came. The lizard came, then the dolphin. We opened our eyes and literally saw the animals. We saw the buffalo on reserves and farms. When we looked into their eyes, we saw they had tremendous teachings to give us. In a world where we are losing it all, they said, "Follow us, look at what you see when you look out of our eyes." We practiced looking out of their eyes and became who we are.

Now the spirit animals will speak to you. They tell us that this teaching is for anyone who wants to follow this path. It is both practical and mystical. When we saw out of the eyes of the bear, he said, "For thousands of years we have been honoring our land.

You are ruining our places in just a few years." The spirit animals have important messages for all of us. In the animal stories, we use *he* or *she*. Your animal can be either he or she; do not worry about how we refer to that particular animal.

The path takes us back to who we once were as humans and it reconnects us to the earth. It reminds us: "I am the mountain. I am the earthquake, the swamp, the river as it floods and recedes. I am the oak that is home to the owl; I am the owl's nest; I am the owl. I am all these things." This kit will show you that you can change your own consciousness and realize who you are now. The power of the animals and the earth is within you. Create the medicine wheel and do this important work.

Owl

Owl was one of the primary power animals from the earliest times of shamanism in Siberia thousands of years ago. Often in the east, brought by the wind, owl comes out of the darkness into dusk or dawn.

Owl takes you deep into your own inner world. The owl can go anywhere. She glides silently on the currents of your own dreams. Just as easily she flies inside the tree trunk or inside your dreams. The owl is a witness in silence and clarity. With owl, you start in a place where you are seen for who you are. Everything about your

life—your dreams, your imagination, your spirit—is seen with clarity. The unconscious becomes revealed. When the owl looks inside us, we understand we can go wherever we desire.

Owl teaches that life is not about being loved unconditionally but rather being seen unconditionally. When owl is present, there is no judgment. She sees with a gaze that is pristine, clear, real, and truthful. Shamans start at the place where they see themselves as they truly are, with clear vision. Nothing hides from owl. Nothing is invisible.

The power of this clarity of vision is great. As owl takes you into her body, you can fly through darkness with precision and grace. The unknown becomes clear. It is as if you become part of the darkness with perfect safety. This perfection in flight, and in life, becomes yours.

With owl, we see beyond death to rebirth. Sometimes people fear owl because they want their vision to stop at death. Owl sees through the veils of death to the other side.

She tells you the legends of the owls, singing to you, "Come through my feathers, go into the darkness. I will show you what lives there, I will show you the world within." Owl brings visions to light, dreams to consciousness.

Let yourself embody the spirit owl. Her way of seeing is deeper than your own, and she will show you how to go there with her. As you see through the eyes of the owl, you see what she sees in the darkness, and you hear what she hears. Go within, travel in silence. In the darkness, truth is revealed.

The essence of the owl is inner vision and the ability to look deep inside ourselves without fear.

Eagle

With eagle we soar to heights that offer vast perspective. As eagle, you will see the landscape, soaring above it, yet still be connected to the earth. The eagle embodies great abundance. He perches on the highest tree atop the highest mountain from where he sees all. With eagle you soar on wind currents that take you up to the sun. You are fearless about being in flight at this height and you share the keenness of eagle's vision. You can see deep into the crevices of the earth and inside its sharp edges.

Eagle is about success, power, and manifestation. Eagle builds a huge nest at a great height. This is the eagle's manifestation of his great vision. As he builds his home, he carries branches and prey from the lowland valley to the highest point that can be reached. As you embody the eagle, you gain swiftness in flight and fearlessness in your dives. The spirit of the eagle unlocks your own ability to fly, dive, free-fall, and soar in pursuit of precisely what you want in life. Eagle can swoop down from above in a dive only to emerge with his prey. He has the power, swiftness, and grace to do this naturally. Eagle says, "Don't be afraid to take the fall, to go high and low, to soar. You will always be successful."

Eagles fly at heights that afford them a horizon of 360 degrees. They are at the top of the medicine wheel axis, and they can see the earth as it rotates below them. They see the entire medicine wheel and everything that happens on earth. If you want to see all the animals, look out of the eyes of the eagle.

Eagle has to do with physical manifestation in the outer world and spiritual manifestation in the spirit world. They experience the medicine wheel as the landscape itself. And from their commanding height, this is their place of power. If you can't find places of power, follow eagle, and he will take you there.

Eagle embodies light as the owl does darkness. Eagle flies to the sun; he represents illumination, showing you in your brightest light.

Eagles even make love in full flight. They fly up in spirals higher and higher, they lock claws and stay together in free fall while mating. Eagles are fearless during this wild, dizzying descent.

They are big, powerful birds, and they will help you harness their power. With their sharp talons they will tear you apart, but this is how you will know the eagle has taken you. Great power does not come without pain. As you become one with the eagle, fly as high as you can. Find the highest mountain, perch on the edge. You too will have tremendous sight, clarity, and awareness of every detail and movement. The eagle within you will manifest your own greatness and greatest accomplishments.

Eagle is at home at this great height. The eagle within you is also at home with your own success and accomplishment. Your voice becomes one with the eagle and you will hear yourself say, "I can fly like eagle, for I see out of his eyes." Follow the eagle, wherever it goes, and he will guide you to your potential.

Eagle told us, "I am regal. I rule the medicine wheel. I carry messages of love between lovers. I link heaven and earth. I carry spirits and prayers to heaven. I create fire, mountains, the tallest trees. I urge you, be imaginative. To be an eagle, listen to the wildest voices within you, for you are truly great."

Eagle is about illumination, about seeing forever in clarity and light.

Lion

Lion is passion, fire, and power. Lion represents the manifestation of love and power in your life. Lions bring lovers together and bind them as one. They will show themselves to lovers, protect them and give them babies. If you want a lover, lion will bring one to you.

Lion calls you. The lion directs your gaze not inward but outward. Lion teaches you to see the truth as it is in the outer world. Lion shows us how to see what is happening and what has happened. Lion lives, with passion and power, in the world as it is.

The lion shows us how to move with elegance and grace. She shows us how to be at home in our body's power.

Lion will help you meet your basic needs and desires, for he gets what he wants. When he relaxes in the full, high-noon sun, he roars with strength and power. He is surrounded by the pride and community, inclusive of old and young, by lovers and babies, and draws his strength from community. The collective energies of the group make hunting possible and fulfill basic needs. The lion lives in balance, resting to conserve energy, yet always ready for the chase. When you see through the eyes of the lion, you will learn to get what you need in life in balance with what surrounds you. This is the lion's strength and passion.

The lion is cool, keen, directive, private. He covers a wide range, and he is independent yet connected. He watches carefully, stalks, pauses, encircles his goal, and then attacks. He often succeeds. When lion walks beside you, you are protected, strong, and empowered. Lion is a manifestation of energy, fearless actualization of forms in the world. Lion is passion in love, power in manifestation.

Lion says, "We have always been lovers. Our spirit can appear to you anywhere and take you. We can show ourselves to you on the roof of your house, in the road in front of your car. We appear in the colors of the sunset, huge and pregnant, telling you that your lover is always with you."

The lion is about strength, passion, and power.

Bear

One of the most powerful animal spirits, the bear means healing.

Bear is called medicine bear, and his healing powers come from deep in the quiet waters of the unconscious, the seat of all healing, dreams, and visions. From that still pool, the bear brings forth your power to heal.

During bear ritual, we become one with the bear and tap into his ability to heal. We wear bearskins, and dance inside the bear's body. The bear is a solitary dancer, aggressive and powerful. Bears are steeped in ceremony and performance. The bear shaman's power fills a room and draws people with his charisma.

With the power to heal comes the responsibility to tend to whatever is sick. Bear teaches us to save the animals and their habitats, to heal the earth and ourselves. When you are the bear shaman, you see out of the eyes of the bear and realize the job before you is immense and important. The bear teaches us humility and responsibility in healing, and being there for the long haul. Bear brings the energy of the earth to create healing—to create harmony and balance in your life.

Bear goes through periods of hibernation, periods of solitary power, when that immense, slumbering body is a full presence in the spirit world. Bears migrate, circle the landscape, move across huge distances, travel, and explore. Bear creates and holds sacred space. The bear shaman is one of the most powerful healers of the medicine wheel, one of the most eloquent teachers of shamanism.

Bear says, "We know the mountains, the rivers, and the salmon. We lead you deep into the wilderness. We are ceremonialists par excellence. We have done shamanic ceremony long before humans were born. We invented shamanism."

Bear is about healing with responsibility.

Turtle

Turtle is the earth. As turtle, you go within the body of the living earth to experience intense grounding. He takes you deeply into your job, your family, your friends, your home. Turtle is about safety, comfort, and protection. Turtle means being taken care of and taking care of others.

The sea turtle is about going deep in the waters of the earth. These waters are its home. Not the dark waters of the unconscious, they are the soft green sea where the sea grasses move with the currents, where you graze in peace. When you are turtle, you are in perfect peace and harmony, maintaining a gentle slowness that is the core of meditation and rest. In the slow, watery environment of the emotions, turtle takes you to the dreamy, secure places within.

Turtle may not seem as romantic as lion's passion for falling in love, but falling in love without grounding is dangerous. Grounding tempers passion. Turtle turns love into life. We embody turtle when we are at home—solid, secure, and stable.

Turtle says, "Slow down. Bring your body close to the ground and see at the level of the grasses. See that each step is one step along your path. My steadfastness will take you deeper into your own body, into the earth. Pause. Make each step sacred and intentional. Experience the fullness of the present." Seeing out of the eyes of the turtle will take you deeper into this shamanic work. Turtle is essential to balance the energies of this work.

Turtle is about being grounded in the body of the living earth.

Serpent

Serpent moves in all directions, sliding easily around the medicine wheel. In ancient traditions, serpents were used in worship, healing, and to invoke the Goddess. When the Goddess rises within you, serpent rises too. Imagine serpent uncoiling toward the sun. Serpent is the tongue of fire and the jagged bolt of lightning. Yet she can take hold of her own tail, forming a perfect circle, or coil with herself or another serpent, at once joined and separate.

When you embody the spirit of the serpent, passion will rise within and set you on fire. She can strike like lightning and transform your future in an instant. She comes from the ground or caves, resonating with the untapped potential energy of the earth. As she surrounds you, she opens her mouth and takes you in whole, only to rebirth you.

The serpent also embodies transformation and renewal. Snakes shed their skins, and emerge as if reborn. When you become serpent, you shed your old self and emerge anew.

Serpents have long been associated with healers, venom medicine, poisons, liniments, magic. They heal, but mishandled, they can kill.

The serpent says, "I am electric, filled with energy. I am the joining of the earth and sky. When your passion rises, I uncoil from the base of your spine, bringing you the power of the goddess to heal, transform, and renew. When you see out of the eyes of the serpent, you shed your old skin and are reborn."

Serpent is about energy rising and rebirth.

Beaver

Careful building is the essence of the beaver. Beavers act with deliberate purpose, cutting down one tree at a time, removing each branch with slow precision. Beavers are steadily productive, and take one step at a time toward completion of the larger job at hand. By doing one thing at a time, they have faith in the completion of their task. They do not hurry, and they know how to rest.

Beaver is in harmony with the ebb and flow of life, letting go and moving on. With their quiet, careful building they have the power to dam a huge river. They can change the course of an entire river or cause a huge lake to form. Beavers control water, one of the most powerful of elements. They are masters of energy. The beaver teaches us about mastery of the flow.

And yet the river always reasserts its power. As we watch the beaver adapt to the changing currents of the river, we learn to use the resources available to us when life changes unexpectedly. Beavers are not displaced by fluctuations of energy; they do not panic but stay focused and rebuild their homes.

The beaver says, "Building and doing is all there is. As waters rise and fall, we build and rebuild, seeking higher ground. Your life is yours, live it fully, put your full energy into building it. We slap our tails on the water. We make the river resound with the noise, but the water is unchanged."

Beaver shaman also teaches us about building a spiritual home. Beaver says that he built the first sweat lodge, a symbol of prayer and hard work. When the beaver built the first sweat lodge, he gathered all the animals together to pray. He honored each one for their work. When we invoke beaver spirit, we build our life from prayer, honoring each part.

The beaver spirit is about commitment and building a full life, one step at a time through prayer.

Lizard, Alligator

Ancient and adaptable, that is lizard. Lizards emerge from the earth, timeless, with prehistoric roots. They are among the most adaptable of all the animals and live in both dry and wet environments. They can walk vertically up the surface of a rock or crawl upside down. Some can even change color, and for this remarkable ability, we call lizard the magician.

Lizard, alligator, and crocodile can slow down their metabolism with a drop in body temperature. They warm and cool themselves in harmony with the earth. They can survive for long periods without food, fasting until food becomes available. Slow moving or still for hours, yet they can react with lightning speed. Lizard is wild and primitive with a deep connection to the earth.

Alligators are not social. They are detached, but not aggressive unless threatened. They are skilled hunters with powerful jaws that can crush bones. Alligator is fierce in the protection of her young.

Lizard says, "We have been here forever. Do not forget us. We were born under the stones of your medicine wheel." When you see out of the eyes of lizard, you are surrounded by an ancient stillness that is timeless and beautiful.

Lizard is about survival and detachment.

Coyote

Coyote is the eternal trickster. In ancient traditions, coyote initiated pranks and silliness. But when coyote comes to you, the message is: Don't take yourself seriously. Despite his clowning, coyote is immensely powerful and helps make things happen. When coyote is involved, things happen in the way you least expect. You get what you want, but don't expect to recognize it at first. Coyote works in mysterious ways. He, too, is a great adaptor and has little to fear.

Coyote is a central figure of many first-nations' stories. Coyote often creates the world. Coyote is sometimes the hero and sometimes the problem. If coyote comes to you, you'll know it, when suddenly a laugh erupts or you make a fool of yourself. You recognize coyote when your wild, chaotic side emerges and you cause a little trouble. Coyote is the clown doctor, the humor healer, the joker, the destroyer and creator. Coyote may trick you, may even turn your

world upside down. But laugh with him and you will have heard his voice.

Coyote says, "I come to all peoples now. I come to you when you least expect it. I am about surprise. You open the door to me when you invoke me. I give you my power of humor. Are you brave enough to invite me in?"

Coyote is about breaking conventions. Coyote is about change, disorder, breaking rules, and creative new thought. Coyote causes an uproar. Coyote says, "Have faith in what you are doing, even when all is crumbling around you. Allow your wild side to emerge, and take yourself less seriously."

Coyote is about not taking yourself seriously while you make and unmake.

Wolf, Dog

The wolf howls at the full moon, the perfect symbol of untamed wilderness. Wolf watches from a distance, patient and still. He is our connection to the wilderness. Unlike the dog, wolf is not submissive to humans. Wolf has a will of his own.

Wolf is wild, untamed, yet lives in a social structure. As wild pack animals, wolves learn to work together to hunt. Wolf makes intricate strategies and communicates with others. He makes his presence known in a territory. He represents the socialization of the group for a purpose. Wolf teaches you about group consciousness and personal power.

We have become domesticated animals, our wild side subdued, our own inner tendency toward the hunt hidden for most of us. But at heart we are predators, hereditary meat eaters. Wolf reminds us of our inner hunter, of our innate wildness, and of howling at the moon in wild places.

We invoke wolf for his wild power. Wolf tells us, "Do not suppress the wild part of you. It is the part that is connected to the earth." Wolf is secretive, reclusive, part of the group, yet alone.

When you see out of the eyes of the wolf, you see the dynamics of relationships. He knows his position in the pack; he knows his boundaries, and with his eyes, you see the nature of behaviors: aggressive, passive, manipulative, and so on. The wolf sees the strategies of human interaction, noting who is in control.

Wolf teaches us to set limits and say no. He says, "I will not let the space around me be taken. I must keep my inner landscape wild. I have my own space. People can't make me do these things. There would be nowhere for me to roam." Wolf is the essence of the untamable wilderness.

Dog is wolf domesticated. The dog has lived with humans for thousands of years. Dog protects us, herds our animals, helps us hunt, befriends us, keeps us company. Dog loves unconditionally. Dogs bring animal spirits into our homes every day. Dog is loyal, true, and submissive. Dog is honest, and dog sees us as we are. Dog is brave in the face of death and teaches us courage when we are ill.

Wolf is about untamed wildness and beauty.

Dog is about loyalty and protection.

Spider

Spider weaves a silver tapestry that connects her to the source of life. Her web comes from inside, and each one is different and complex. Building continuously, spider weaves art, symmetry, and beauty. Spider is the architect, the artist, the Creator, the one who captures evanescent beauty. Her art comes and goes in concert with her surroundings: invisible at night, illuminated with diamonds from the morning dew, or washed away by a storm.

Spider hangs suspended, waiting for what comes to her. She sits perfectly still and waits until her food comes, then wraps it up, saving it for later. Spider is about resourcefulness and holding on to what you need. Spider means building, creating, and waiting. Spider is about faith.

She looks deep into the center of the universe, and from the center you can see the energy go up into her legs. Her web is the fabric of your own life. She catches energy and power, and weaves it into the web. If you look closely, you can see that she is weaving a spiral of light from exploding nebulae that come from the inner depths.

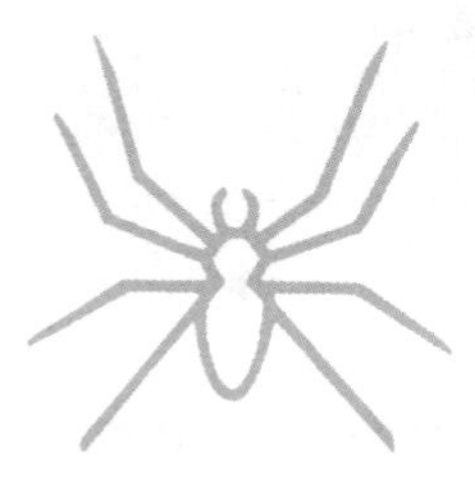

She says, "As I make the web, I bring it to each one of you and weave it into your heart. Each strand goes from me to you, up into the center of your heart. You are in the place where time and space are not limited and these threads spiral to infinity, into the past, present, and the future." Spider holds the interlocking connections together.

When you see out of the eyes of spider, you can see the silver threads that flow out of your heart as you make the connections that join you to life. Threads connect you to your family, to the people you work with, and to the larger web that connects you to the whole world. Spider shows you the layers of webs woven in your life. The web expands and contracts, the web floats and is as large as the universe. Each thread you weave flows from your own heart to someone else, creating connections of webs. Some are small, like your family, while some are large, like your medicine wheel. In the weaving of any web, even the simplest one, it is always connected to the web of the universe.

Spider weaves the web of life. Spider is about connections.

Ant

Even the tiny ant has a place in the medicine wheel. Her message is subtle and sometimes easily overlooked, but she has much to share with us. When she appears, like when we are on a picnic, she is often an unwanted guest.

Ant has burrowed beneath the earth for millenia. Among the most successful and adaptable creatures we know, she represents community, perseverance, and strength.

As you watch the diminutive ant carry something twice her size, draw strength from her example. She comes to you for one small crumb of food, which she will haul back to the nest. Ant's social order is complex and a model of efficiency. One is a brave scout, sent out to explore. Soon, the next one follows with a clear sense of purpose and absolute trust. They work as a team and accomplish huge tasks. Ant helps us see how our role in life is to be a scout or a follower, depending on the situation.

Ant forces us to pay careful attention to the small things beneath our feet. Her teachings are as complex as the tunnels in her nest. Ant says, "You can't get rid of ants; accept your world."

Ant is about paying attention and being yourself with your community.

Deer

Of all the animals in the medicine wheel, deer is perhaps the most gentle, graceful, and beautiful. They move slowly with a delicate step. Deer is the manifestation of beauty and prosperity. When you see a deer, it is an omen of good things. Usually they surprise you with their sudden appearance on the side of the road, or at the top of a rise.

Because of their gentle demeanor, they are easily hunted. They have a keen sense of attention, and are on the alert for danger. They have always provided food, clothing, and shelter for people, and the deer's whole body is used in ceremony. Deer has given us much to be thankful for. Deer gives us the gifts of beauty, agility, and grace.

In the medicine wheel, deer runs in spirals of ecstasy with their agility and swiftness. Deer sets the medicine wheel spinning, turning it into a dance. They run in wild spirals around the burial mounds, and the power places. Ceremonial dancing deer are the keepers of the sacred sites.

Deer will bring spirals of beauty to your life.

Horse

Horse is the vehicle. Horse takes you into the wilderness, far into yourself. Horse looks you in the eye and shows you the nature of the large animals.

Horse was one of the first animals to be in partnership with humans. He makes us four legged and fleet. For many peoples, horse changed everything. Suddenly they could travel fast and far.

Horses are social animals made to be with each other, to support each other. Among horses there are leaders and followers. A leader horse will take you into the spirit world.

When we make a medicine wheel with the horse, he can bring us on a journey or assist us with hard work. Horse is good for people in relationships and on a journey. Horse is strong and brings prosperity too. They do work but need work put into them. Horse embodies nurturing and also being taken care of.

Horse will travel with you into the land of the spirits too. Horse takes you there so you can do work, so you can see, so you can receive his gifts. Horse is the vehicle to be given a vision. Horse is beautiful. Horse's body is strong, majestic, lithe, smooth. A companion and friend, horse takes you to your deepest love.

Horse brings you where you need to go in life. Horse is the symbol of the tamed spirit that we use. But remember, horse has been deeply abused. Horse has power and the human has conquered it. With horse, we must deal with issues of human domination and control. Horse teaches us to find the space where you deeply honor the power of the other instead of being afraid of it. Thus, horse and the rider can become one as equals with respect for each.

Horse is about traveling and doing work in both worlds.

Buffalo

The teaching of the buffalo was specific. To some people, it was, and still is, the most sacred teaching. Buffalo says, "I am the food. I am the nurturing mother. I am the true earth mother, she who takes care of it all. I stand for all the support animals that make the earth. I am not the hunter. I give myself to you to feed you and clothe you and give you shelter. I support your entire spirit world." Buffalo makes you whole and gives you great wealth.

Buffalo has almost been exterminated, and it now takes effort to find buffalo teaching. Go to them and acknowledge the scarcity of what was once abundant. The passing of the buffalo also meant the near extermination of a whole people. Buffalo reminds us, "What was once plentiful is now scarce."

First-nations people have many sacred buffalo stories, and one of the most powerful is the legend of the white buffalo. The birth of the white buffalo was an event as important to some people as the coming of Christ. It was predicted and it has happened. This is the story of the birth of the white buffalo as told to us when we visited her farm.

"Long ago there was hunger and war. Two men went in each direction to find game. One pair saw a woman on a hilltop. They went to her, and one man asked her to make love. She turned him into a skeleton in a cloud of white smoke. She said to the other man, 'Come here, I won't hurt you. Take me to your village.' She gave his people ceremony, the medicine bundle, the sacred pipe, tobacco. She brought them game. Before she left, she turned into a white buffalo, and said, 'When I return as the white buffalo, there will be harmony, peace, and plenty for everyone.'

"White buffalo woman said, 'I will be born on a white man's land, in the center of North America. I will be white when I am born, and then I will turn the colors of the directions, and of the four races: white, black, red, and yellow. I will turn white again in my fifth year and then peace will come to the earth.' The white buffalo changed colors each year, as prophesied. Obviously, the coming of the white buffalo did not immediately create world peace. The first-nations peoples believe that it is a spiritual event and has changed spiritual space. Peace will come, now that the white buffalo calf is born. When the white buffalo was born on August 20, 1994, in Wisconsin, the war in Central America finally ceased and peace returned. Now people come from all over to visit her, elders do ceremony with her. On her birthday, 750 people come. People pray, leave medicine bundles, and tie feathers on the fence around her pen. You can visit white buffalo and bring her an offering just as we did."

Buffalo is about feeding, clothing, and housing the world with abundance.

Dolphin, Whale

Dolphins are communicators, guides, and friends from a different element. When they come to you, you are entranced and taken to a place closer to spirit. Dolphins are at home in the vast, boundless ocean, a world unto itself.

The waves of the ocean are the rhythm of Her heartbeat. Dolphin rides on the inner heartbeat of the living earth. They are pure nature and help us to find our essence when we are with them. They teach that it is not about what you have or what is around you, but rather what you give.

Dolphin and whale are about immersion into the vast waters, deep in our consciousness. Dolphin is the eternal dreamer, swimming in grace. They go deep and ascend to the surface. As the dolphin looks into your eyes, you will know that all creatures are your friends; they bring you love from the other side.

You can give dolphin your greatest sorrow. She will take it to the bottom of the sea, and leave it in the abyss. Dolphins are guardians who accompany spirits on their journey to the other side. Give dolphin an offering, and she will save your life.

Dolphin is about communication and being who you are without your material objects.

Man, Woman, Child

The ancient ones may come to you as guides in the form of a man, woman, or child. They can be old, middle-aged, young, or even a baby. They are all different ancestral guides, representing the grandfather and grandmother spirits. They live in the old-growth trees in the circles formed by the growth rings. They walk toward you and present themselves to you in nature. They will come in silence.

Depending on his age, a man as a guide can mean many things. Often he will come to solve problems. He penetrates and exhibits power and control. The old man can be about wisdom, knowledge, about being alone. Middle-aged man is about building or seeking wisdom, or going on quests for enlightenment. Young man is about enthusiasm, energy, and hope.

A woman guide may come as a young girl, a mother, or a crone. She is about ancient knowledge, seeing deep into the spirit world, and healing. Woman represents Mother Earth and goddesses. She reveals various aspects within us simultaneously. She gives birth, she is receptive. She is about the sensual and soft. She is about service and nurturing the earth.

Man goes into the sun fearlessly, but woman sees deeper in the darkness. Man acts, woman sees and hears. Man takes over and controls. Woman nurtures and empowers. Together they are very powerful. These stories are about aspects of energy, not about gender.

Child is about tenderness, innocence, perfection, and mischievousness. Dependency goes hand in hand with learning, rapid change with forgiveness. The child is about faith and natural process. Children are trusting, flexible, and represent the future.

The ancient ones see the world of the past in the present. With them, you can see out of the eyes of the ones who came before you, the ancestral spirits who are the guardians of earth. You become an ancient one here in the present. Anyone who does this work shares the wisdom and energy of those who speak from the past.

The ancient ones tell us: "You are our living voice. Remember the time when we were one with the earth. We were one people, with no separation."

Man and woman are about oneness and the wisdom of ancient experience.

Appendix: Resources

There are many resources you can use to enrich your experience of making medicine wheels and being a shaman.

You can use the medicine wheels that have been built and used forever. These medicine wheels are not just archeological structures, they are living sacred sites that are full of energy.

Through the ages, shamans have built great medicine wheels all over the earth. Stonehenge and Avebury, in England, are beautiful stone circles that are believed to have functioned as astronomical observatories as well as sites for sacred ritual. In Great Britain are the ley lines of energy that go through "serpent sites" all through southern England. Delos and Delphi in Greece each have sacred springs and caves and places where the oracle was visited on pilgrimages. Tinos, Greece, has the sacred spring of the Virgin, as does Lourdes in France. The Australian dreamtime maps are paintings and legends of the entire landscape as a sacred medicine wheel complete with animal and spirit stories.

In North America, She Who Watches on the Columbia River near Dales, Oregon, is the face of She who gardens us from above that was worshiped in sacred ritual. Chaco Canyon, Aztec Ruin, Canyon De Chelley, in the southwest United States are immense sites that were used for ritual for thousands of years. In Florida, the Crystal River mounds and the huge, newly discovered Miami circle are both sacred medicine wheels of the ancient ones. The medicine wheels in Montana and Alberta, Canada, are stone circles that were used as burial mounds and places of sacred ritual.

Chances are there is a medicine wheel near you. You can find it by looking on the World Wide Web under the place you want to go and the search words "sacred sites, mounds, medicine wheels, Native American," or by looking at maps for the sign of a ruin or archeological site. You can read books on sacred sites and look at Web sites on traveling to sacred sites. Many travel companies now have tours of sacred sites, and you can see by their itinerary where popular sites are.

Ritual Medicine Wheel Pilgrimages

Here are examples of large medicine wheels that you can do as pilgrimages. You can also go to the site to make a smaller wheel at the site itself. For example, you can go to Avebury and make a medicine wheel within one stone circle that goes from east to south to west to north around the circle itself. A medicine wheel can be any size, from your own personal wheel on a table to the whole earth or universe in your mind's eye.

Great Britain: England has ley lines, sacred lines that go from the western end at Cornwall to the east coast north of London. They go through Mount St. Michael, Glastonbury Tor, Avebury and its barrow, and Tor, and pass many springs. You can make a medicine wheel from the west at the Men An Tor stone to the east wherever you land, with Avebury to the south, and the horse at the north.

Chaco Canyon: Make a medicine wheel with Chaco in the center; you can make Taos or Sante Fe on the east, Zuni at the south, Canyon De Chelly at the west, and Aztec Ruin at the north.

The serpent mound in Ohio: You can make a medicine wheel on the mound itself or to surrounding mounds in each direction.

She Who Watches, in Dales, Oregon: The medicine wheel can be around the petroglyph, to the Columbia River, to the falls, and to the ocean.

Florida mounds: The medicine wheel can be from the bear corridor in Cedar Key Forest to the west; springs in the north, the turtle migration sites on the beaches; in the south, the lion panther at Great Cypress Swamp; and in the east, the owl at Crescent Beach.

In Greece you can make the medicine wheel extend from Delos in the east at the sacred cave of Artemis; to Delphi in the west, to the omphale of the oracle; to Tinos in the north, to the sacred spring; to Athens in the south, to the owl at the Parthenon.

In San Francisco you can make the medicine wheel from Mount Tamalpais in the west, to Muir Woods in the south, to the Pacific Ocean in the west, and the Miwok village in the north.

In Alberta and Montana you can make a medicine wheel from Montana's great wheel in the south to Buffalo Jump in the east to the mountains in the west (where the bear lives) to the medicine wheels near Calgary in the north.

There are many books and Web sites about medicine wheels and shamanism. Our site, <http://www.pathofthefeather.com> will start you off. Our links page has connections to other sites dealing with medicine wheels, sacred sites, shamanism, and sacred travel.

Some Sites We Recommend

"Aboriginal Rock Paintings"
<http://www.lights.com/waterways/arch/rockart.htm>

"The Ancient Sites Directory," stone circles
<http://www.henge.demon.co.uk/index.html>

"Angela Corelis—Symbolism Used by the Huichols"
<http://www.mexconnect/mex_/huichol/ab_th~3.htm>

Animal spirit cards
<http://www.spiritcards.com>

"Animal Spirit Energies"
<http://www.soultones.com/totems.html>

"The Bear Den Photo Gallery"
<http://www.nature-net.com/bears/gallery.html>

"Bighorn Medicine Wheel 3: How They Work (SK 8)"
<http://indy4.fdl.cc.mn.us/~isk/stars/starkno8.html>

Contemporary medicine wheel
<http://www.geo.org>

"Diamondback Rattlesnake"
<http://www.lsjunction.com/images/rattler.htm>

"Dusters Native American White Buffalo Page"
<http://www.specent.com/~duster/volc4.html>

"Every Animal There Is"
<http://www3.ns.sympatico.ca/educate/animal.htm>

"Hopi Message for Mankind"
<http://hinduismtoday.kauai.hi.us/ashram/Resources/Hopi/techqua_ikachi.html>

"Information on Owls" the natural history of the barred owl
<http://www.rci.rutgers.edu/~au/owl.htm>

"McNeil River State Game Sanctuary:Visitor Information"
<http://www.state.ak.us/local/akpages/FISH.GAME/wildlife/region2/refuge2/mr-info.htm>

"Miracle Buffalo American Indian Story"
<http://indy4.fdl.cc.mn.us/~isk/arvol/whitbuff.html>
Mound builders
<http://ngeorgia.com/cgibin/links/moundbuilders>
"Mystery of the Medicine Wheels"
<http://www.usask.ca/education/ideas/tplan/sslp/wheel/medicine.htm>
"Outdoor Recreation in Katmai National Park, Alaska Peninsula; Fishing, Hunting, Rafting, Backcountry Camping"
<http://www.vacationalaska.com/info/publiclands/katmai.html>
"The Owl Pages"
<http://www.owlpages.com/index.html>
"Power Animals: Keywords and Descriptions for Some Important Power Animals"
<http://rainbowcrystal.com/power/powerdef.html>
Rock art
<http://www.geocities.com/Tokyo/2384/links.html>
"Scorpions Found in Florida, Florida Gators, Snakes"
<http://www.gate.net/~critter/critter5.htm>
"Sea Turtle Survival League/Caribbean Conservation Corporation," dedicated to the preservation of sea turtles and other wildlife
<http://www.cccturtle.org>
"Shamanism: Working with Animal Spirits, Core Shamanism"
<http://www.geocities.com/RainForest/4076/Books.html>
"Star Knowledge 5, Bighorn Medicine Wheel," animal totems
<http://indy4.fdl.cc.mn.us/~isk/stars/starkno5.html>
"Stone Pages—A Guide to European Megaliths"
<http://www.stonepages.com/HomEng.html>
Totem animals
<http://www60.pair.com/spiritln/totem2.html>
"Wolfsong"
<http://PersonalWebs.myriad.net/wolfsong/wolfsong.htm>

Recommended Reading

Eliade, Mircea. *Shamanism: Archaic Techniques of Ecstasy.* 2nd ed. Translated by Willard R. Trask. Princeton: Princeton University Press, 1972.

Halifax, Joan. *Shamanic Voices: A Survey of Visionary Narratives.* New York: Dutton, 1979.

Harner, Michael. *The Way of the Shaman.* 10th anniversary ed. San Francisco: HarperSanFrancisco, 1990.

About the Authors

Michael Samuels, M.D., and Mary Rockwood Lane, Ph.D., are living the Path of the Feather and have had the experiences they shared in this book. The stories of the ancient ones and the animal spirits have been told to them and they will tell them to you. They have both had extensive experiences with spirit guides, spirit animals, and medicine wheels. They have done rituals all over the world and have documented them in photography and poetry that they share with patients, artists, and healers in workshops and lectures.

Michael Samuels, M.D., has used art and guided imagery with cancer patients for over twenty-five years in private practice and in consultation. He has developed a practice where some patients use shamanic imagery and take the Path of the Feather. He uses spirit animals with patients with many illnesses including cancer. He has watched as his patients have done ritual, drawn, played music, and written themselves well. He is on the advisory boards of Commonweal, and Tamalpa

Institute, an organization that uses dance for healing. He is also the founder and director of Art as a Healing Force, a project started in 1990 devoted to making art and healing one. He lectures and does workshops nationwide for physicians, nurses, artists, and patients on how to use art in healing and on medicine wheels and spirit animals. He has organized many nationwide conferences on art and healing and visits and participates in projects in hospitals where art and music are used with patients. He leads workshops on shamanic healing, and works with patients, healers, and artists in using the Path of the Feather. He networks people in the field together and is a recognized leader in art and healing.

He is the author of fifteen books including the best-selling *Well Body Book, Well Baby Book, Well Pregnancy Book,* and *Seeing with the Mind's Eye.* With Mary Rockwood Lane, he has written *Creative Healing, How Art, Writing, Dance and Music Can Heal Body and Soul,* and *Spirit Healing.* He lives in Bolinas, California, and has two grown sons.

MARY ROCKWOOD LANE, PH.D., is a painter and a nurse. She is the cofounder and codirector of the Arts in Medicine program at University of Florida, Gainesville, and founded their artist-in-residence program. She has led and developed that program for over seven years. Her Ph.D. dissertation in nursing from the University of Florida, Gainesville, was on her patient's lived experience of art and healing. It was the first advanced degree in art and healing in the medical field. In her program she employs shamanic processes with patients and artists. She has written many articles on art and healing in nursing and medical journals and is a recognized leader in the field. She lectures and teaches workshops on art and healing and on the Path of the Feather across the world and helps medical centers and artists set up art-and-healing programs. She is coauthor, with Michael Samuels, of *Creative Healing* and *Spirit Healing.* She lives in Gainesville, Florida, and has three children.